KT-590-250

GCSE English

Dr Jekyll & Mr Hyde

by Robert Louis Stevenson

Jekyll and Hyde — probably the greatest double-act in English literature. But writing essays about the novel? That can be a challenge.

Not to worry. This brilliant Text Guide explains the whole thing — characters, language, themes, historical background... the lot. And because it's a CGP book, we get straight to the point, with no needless rambling.

We've also included plenty of practice questions to test you on what you've learned, plus advice on how to plan and write brilliant answers in the exams! It's enough to make you feel like a completely different person.

The Text Guide

CONTENTS

CONTENTS

The Characters in 'Dr Jekyll and Mr Hyde'
'Dr Jekyll and Mr Hyde' Cartoon

Published by CGP

Editors:
Emma Bonney
Alex Fairer
Heather Gregson

Contributor:
Jane Harrison

With thanks to Claire Boulter and Elisabeth Quincey for the proofreading.
With thanks to Jan Greenway for the copyright research.

Acknowledgements:

Cover image and image on page 4 - Cobble stone © ROMAOSLO/iStockphoto.com

With thanks to akg-images for permission to use the image on page 5.

With thanks to Alamy for permission to use the images on pages 1, 3, 12, 17, 37 & 38

With thanks to Getty Images for permission to use the image on page 2.

With thanks to iStockphoto.com for permission to use the image on page 7.

With thanks to Mary Evans Picture Library for permission to use the images on pages 6 & 8.

With thanks to Neil Hastings for permission to use the image on page 3.

With thanks to Nick Collinge @ Love It Studios for permission to use the images on pages 3, 4, 5, 10, 13, 14, 15, 16, 19, 20, 22, 24, 25, 26, 27, 28, 29, 33, 34, 35, 36, 42, 43, 45 & 47.
Images from Barrow Operatic and Dramatic Society's 2014 production of 'Jekyll & Hyde'.

With thanks to Photofest Digital for permission to use the images on pages 3, 11, 18, 23, 44, 46 & 48.

Every effort has been made to locate copyright holders and obtain permission to reproduce sources.
For those sources where it has been difficult to trace the copyright holder of the work, we would be grateful
for information. If any copyright holder would like us to make an amendment to the acknowledgements,
please notify us and we will gladly update the book at the next reprint. Thank you.

ISBN: 978 1 78294 308 2
Printed by Elanders Ltd, Newcastle upon Tyne.
Clipart from Corel®

Based on the classic CGP style created by Richard Parsons.

Text, design, layout and original illustrations © Coordination Group Publications Ltd. (CGP) 2015
All rights reserved.

Photocopying more than one chapter of this book is not permitted. Extra copies are available from CGP.
0800 1712 712 • www.cgpbooks.co.uk

Introduction to 'Jekyll and Hyde' and Stevenson

'Jekyll and Hyde' is about man's dual nature

- The novel is about a <u>respectable</u> doctor, called Henry <u>Jekyll</u>, who transforms into the <u>evil</u> Edward <u>Hyde</u>.

- Although it's <u>fictional</u>, the novel reflects the <u>strict values</u> of Victorian society, in which people were expected to be <u>restrained</u> and <u>appear respectable</u> at all times.

> *Jekyll and Hyde* has a strong message
>
> 1) *Jekyll and Hyde* is about <u>human nature</u> — <u>everyone</u> has good and evil inside them.
>
> 2) If people <u>explore</u> their dark side, it can lead to <u>problems</u> — but <u>hiding</u> or <u>denying</u> it leads to problems <u>too</u>.

© The Art Archive / Alamy

Robert Louis Stevenson was interested in man's different sides

- As a child, Stevenson was <u>influenced</u> by the <u>strict Christian beliefs</u> of his <u>nanny</u>, Alison Cunningham.

- As an adult, Stevenson was <u>interested</u> in the <u>behaviour</u> of Victorian gentlemen — the way they maintained an outwardly <u>respectable appearance</u>, but <u>secretly</u> indulged in <u>immoral</u> behaviour.

- Stevenson was particularly <u>fascinated</u> by the life of <u>Deacon Brodie</u>, a <u>respectable</u> cabinet maker who led a <u>secret</u> life as a <u>robber</u>.

1850	Born in <u>Edinburgh</u>.
1867	Went to <u>Edinburgh University</u> to study <u>engineering</u>.
1871	Wanted to become a <u>writer</u>, but decided to study <u>law</u> first on his father's advice.
1873	<u>Quarrelled</u> with his father about <u>religion</u> — his father was <u>upset</u> that Stevenson had become an <u>atheist</u>.
1878	Published his <u>first novel</u>, 'An Inland Voyage'.
1880	<u>Married</u> Fanny Osbourne.
1886	Published '<u>The Strange Case of Dr Jekyll and Mr Hyde</u>'.
1889	Moved to <u>Samoa</u> and never returned to Britain.
1894	<u>Died</u>, aged 44.

© Ivy Close Images / Alamy

Background Information

'Jekyll and Hyde' is set in London

Here are the <u>key locations</u> in the novel:

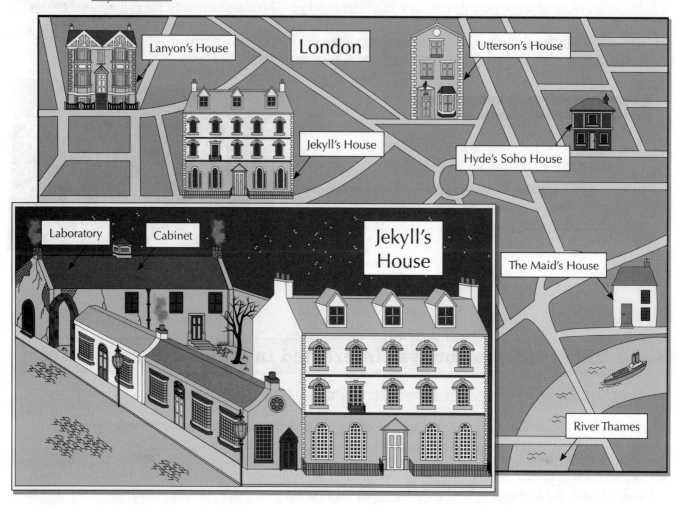

Victorian gentlemen tried to hide their darker side

Mid-19th-century gentlemen

- In Victorian middle and <u>upper-class</u> society, it was important to look <u>respectable</u>. As a result, people <u>hid</u> their <u>true</u> <u>feelings</u>, especially if these were <u>immoral</u> or improper.

- <u>Reputation</u> was <u>very important</u> to Victorian <u>gentlemen</u>. If they were seen doing anything which wasn't respectable, their good name would be <u>ruined</u>.

- To <u>protect</u> their reputation, people often kept their sinful behaviour and less respectable desires <u>secret</u>.

- They didn't like to <u>talk</u> about anything that might <u>damage</u> their <u>reputation</u> or upset their apparently <u>civilised</u> society.

Introduction

Who's Who in 'Jekyll and Hyde'

Dr Henry Jekyll...

...is a well-respected doctor and scientist. He starts to act strangely and stops seeing his friends when he secretly experiments with his alter ego.

Jekyll and Hyde are the same person.

Mr Edward Hyde...

...is the evil side of Jekyll. He's a violent and merciless character who makes people feel uneasy and disgusted.

Mr Gabriel Utterson...

...is a lawyer and Jekyll's friend. He is very rational and sets out to solve the mystery of Jekyll's odd behaviour.

Dr Hastie Lanyon...

...is also a doctor. He used to be close friends with Jekyll, but they fell out over Jekyll's controversial scientific ideas.

Mr Richard Enfield...

...is Utterson's relative and friend. They enjoy spending time together, even though they don't have much in common.

Poole...

...is Jekyll's butler. He's worked for Jekyll for 20 years and knows him well. He's concerned by Jekyll's strange behaviour.

Sir Danvers Carew...

...is an elderly gentleman and Member of Parliament.

Mr Guest...

...is Utterson's clerk. He notices that Hyde's handwriting is almost identical to Jekyll's.

'Jekyll and Hyde' — Plot Summary

© ROMAOSLO/iStockphoto.com

'Jekyll and Hyde'... what happens when?

Here's a little recap of the <u>main events</u> of *Jekyll and Hyde*. It's a good idea to learn what happens when, so that you know exactly how the plot progresses and how all the important events fit together.

Chapters One to Three — the mysterious Mr Hyde

© Nick Collinge @ Love It Studios

- <u>Utterson</u> and <u>Enfield</u> walk past a <u>neglected building</u> which reminds Enfield of a <u>crime</u> in which a man named <u>Hyde</u> trampled a young girl.

- Enfield explains that he put <u>pressure</u> on Hyde to pay for his crime. Hyde went into the building and came out with a <u>cheque</u> signed by <u>Dr Henry Jekyll</u>.

- Utterson is <u>concerned</u> by Jekyll's <u>will</u>, which leaves everything to <u>Hyde</u>. He visits <u>Lanyon</u> and discovers that he and Jekyll have <u>fallen out</u>.

- Utterson meets Hyde and really <u>dislikes</u> him. It turns out that the building Hyde went into when Enfield saw him is the <u>laboratory</u> at <u>Jekyll's home</u>. Utterson concludes that Hyde is <u>blackmailing</u> Jekyll.

- Utterson attends a <u>dinner party</u> thrown by Jekyll. Utterson <u>questions</u> Jekyll about Hyde, but Jekyll asks him to let the matter drop. Jekyll makes Utterson <u>promise</u> that he'll carry out the <u>instructions</u> in his will.

Chapters Four to Five — the disappearance of Mr Hyde

- A year later, a maid witnesses the <u>violent murder</u> of <u>Sir Danvers Carew</u> by <u>Hyde</u>. Utterson takes the police to <u>Hyde's home</u> in <u>Soho</u> where they find the murder weapon. Hyde is <u>nowhere</u> to be found.

- Utterson goes to see <u>Jekyll</u>, who looks <u>very ill</u>. Jekyll claims that he'll <u>never</u> see Hyde again and shows Utterson a <u>letter</u> from <u>Hyde</u> which backs this up.

- However, Utterson is <u>concerned</u> when <u>Poole</u> tells him that <u>no letters</u> had been <u>delivered</u> to the house that morning.

- Later, Utterson shows <u>Guest</u> the letter, who points out the <u>similarity</u> between the <u>handwriting</u> of <u>Jekyll</u> and <u>Hyde</u>.

© Nick Collinge @ Love It Studios

Chapters Six to Eight — Jekyll is in trouble

- There's still <u>no sign</u> of Hyde, and <u>Jekyll</u> becomes more like his <u>old self</u>. But a few months later he hides himself away from his friends again.

- Utterson visits <u>Lanyon</u>, who's <u>very ill</u>. Lanyon <u>refuses</u> to talk about <u>Jekyll</u>. He says he's had a <u>terrible shock</u> and expects to <u>die</u> soon.

- <u>Jekyll</u> writes to Utterson to say that he can't see his friends any more. Lanyon <u>dies</u> and leaves <u>Utterson</u> a <u>letter</u> to be read <u>after</u> Jekyll's death or disappearance.

- Utterson and Enfield walk past Jekyll's house and see <u>Jekyll</u> sitting in the <u>window</u>. They invite him out for a walk, but a <u>sudden</u> look of <u>terror</u> comes across his face and he <u>quickly shuts</u> the window.

- <u>Poole</u> comes to Utterson's house because he's very <u>worried</u> about <u>Jekyll</u>. They go to Jekyll's <u>laboratory</u> and <u>shout</u> to Jekyll, but the voice that responds sounds like <u>Hyde</u>.

- They <u>break in</u> and discover <u>Hyde</u> dead on the floor, having <u>poisoned</u> himself. There's <u>no sign</u> of <u>Jekyll</u>. A <u>letter</u> on the desk addressed to <u>Utterson</u> tells him to read <u>Lanyon's letter</u> and then <u>Jekyll's confession</u>.

Chapters Nine to Ten — the mystery is solved

- <u>Lanyon's letter</u> explains that <u>Hyde</u> drank the <u>potion</u> and <u>transformed</u> into <u>Jekyll</u> in front of him. The <u>shock</u> that Jekyll and Hyde are the <u>same person</u> caused Lanyon's <u>death</u>.

- <u>Jekyll's confession</u> reveals that he had turned into Hyde without meaning to in the park. He wrote to Lanyon, asking for his <u>help</u> to <u>retrieve</u> the ingredients he needed for his potion.

- Jekyll writes that he came from a <u>respectable</u> family, but he was <u>ashamed</u> of his <u>darker</u> desires.

- He created a <u>drug</u> that allowed him to <u>transform</u> between <u>Jekyll</u>, his <u>original self</u>, and <u>Hyde</u>, his <u>purely evil</u> side.

- As time went on, Jekyll started to turn into Hyde <u>without</u> taking the drug.

- He eventually <u>ran out</u> of drugs, which meant that he would become Hyde <u>permanently</u>.

That Henry Jekyll — he's so two-faced...

It's a shame we couldn't all have an alter ego — I'd get mine to do all my revision. *Jekyll and Hyde* is a short novel, but there's still a fair bit to get your teeth into — context, themes, writer's techniques...If you're still not 100% clear on the plot, turn to the back of the book for the cartoon.

Victorian Gentlemen

Stevenson published *Jekyll and Hyde* in 1886, when Queen Victoria was on the throne. The novel will make far more sense if you know a bit about that period in history. If only there was a section to... oh! Look!

'Jekyll and Hyde' is about a group of gentlemen

1) The 'gentleman' was an <u>important figure</u> in Victorian society.

2) A man's <u>social class</u> was one part of being a gentleman — gentlemen were from the <u>upper-classes</u> of Victorian society.

3) His <u>profession</u> was also important — army officers, church ministers, doctors and lawyers might all be counted as gentlemen. Some middle-class men (such as bankers and successful merchants) also <u>aspired</u> to be gentlemen.

© Illustrated London News Ltd / Mary Evans

4) Gentlemen were expected to have <u>strong morals</u> and be <u>kind</u>, particularly towards poorer people. But plenty of people saw this as a <u>less important</u> part of being a gentleman.

5) Being a gentleman brought many <u>benefits</u>. It gave you a chance to enter well-paid professions like <u>medicine</u> and <u>law</u>, and gain the <u>respect</u> of <u>rich clients</u>.

6) It was also important for your <u>children</u>. A gentleman could use his contacts to arrange good marriages for his daughters and well-paid jobs for his sons.

Character — Utterson

Utterson, a successful lawyer, is a <u>good example</u> of the Victorian gentleman.

Gentlemen were obsessed with their reputations

1) Gentlemen were determined to maintain their <u>reputations</u> — without a good reputation, a man couldn't be considered a gentleman at all.

2) Gentlemen would often <u>walk</u> through public places, such as Hyde Park in London. This helped them to keep up their <u>appearance</u> as gentlemen. Utterson and Mr Enfield go on these walks regularly.

3) Gentlemen were expected to keep their <u>emotions</u> under <u>strict control</u>. This forced them to <u>hide their desires</u> for things like sex and alcohol.

Theme — Reputation

Utterson wants to discover the truth about Hyde, but he is <u>worried</u> that it might damage Jekyll's reputation. This <u>slows him down</u> when he is trying solve the mystery. See page 33.

Theme — Dual Nature of Man

Jekyll <u>struggles</u> with the social pressure to be respectable. He "concealed" his "pleasures", but this made him feel like a "<u>double dealer</u>", even before he created Hyde.

4) Many gentlemen were <u>publicly snobbish</u> about disreputable places, like public houses and brothels, whilst visiting them <u>secretly</u> at night. Stevenson hints at this <u>hypocrisy</u> in the novel (see p.34).

5) They were prepared to pay large sums of money to keep activities like these <u>private</u>, which made them vulnerable to <u>blackmail</u>. Utterson assumes that Jekyll is being blackmailed about something in his past. Even Hyde, who doesn't need to protect his reputation, is prepared to pay money, partly to avoid a public <u>scandal</u>.

KEY QUOTE

"I had been safe of all men's respect, wealthy, beloved"

To be a Victorian gent: keep conversation controlled, appearance perfect and immoral activities under the rug. And, you know, don't invent a potion that transforms you into a murderous, ape-like being of pure evil.

Victorian London

If you're thinking Victorian London was all a walk in the park, think again. Sadly, top hats and tail coats were a world away from the poverty experienced by many working-class Londoners. Oh, how the other half live...

Working-class London was overcrowded

1) Whilst the middle and upper-classes lived in <u>richly-furnished houses</u> (like Jekyll's house, which has "a great air of wealth and comfort"), this <u>wasn't</u> true of <u>everyone</u>.

2) The <u>Industrial Revolution</u> meant that many working-class people <u>migrated</u> to large towns and cities to live and work.

3) Housing had to be built <u>rapidly</u> to accommodate workers and their families. Large areas of <u>slums</u> — heavily populated areas of poor quality housing — sprang up in London's <u>East End</u>.

4) Slum housing was generally of a <u>poor quality</u> because it was built so <u>quickly</u>. Whole families could live in one or two <u>rooms</u>. Houses were often <u>damp</u>, with <u>no running water</u> or proper <u>sanitation</u>. This led to widespread outbreaks of fatal <u>diseases</u>, like cholera.

© iStockphoto.com/duncan1890

Writer's Techniques — Setting

In parts of the novel, London could seem <u>nightmarish</u> — the fog and gloom are <u>thick</u> and <u>powerful</u>.

5) The streets in the slums were <u>narrow</u> and <u>poorly lit</u>. Victorian London was known for its <u>smoke</u>, caused by burning coal on a large scale. The East End slums were built close to <u>factories</u> so that people could easily work long hours. This meant that the slums suffered particularly from <u>pollution</u>.

Working-class London was not respectable

1) There were some parts of London where most respectable men <u>wouldn't</u> want to be <u>seen</u>, such as the working-class <u>slums</u>. They also wouldn't want to be seen visiting <u>brothels</u> or <u>public houses</u>.

2) Hyde is <u>associated</u> with these less respectable parts of the city. His house is in a "<u>dismal quarter of Soho</u>", where "<u>ragged children</u>" huddle in doorways.

Theme — Dual Nature of Man

It's not only the characters who are divided in the novel — this theme also applies to the <u>settings</u>. Jekyll's home has two <u>very different</u> entrances, but they both lead to the <u>same</u> building.

Writer's Techniques — The Gothic Novel

Traditionally, Gothic novels were set in <u>faraway</u> places, such as abandoned castles in foreign countries. Stevenson chose to set his story in a place very <u>familiar</u> to his readers, which might make the novel more <u>frightening</u>.

3) But the two sides of the city did <u>overlap</u>. Some gentlemen would deliberately travel to the "dismal" areas of London (where there was less chance of being <u>recognised</u>) to <u>satisfy</u> the desires they <u>hid</u> in public. Jekyll takes this one step <u>further</u> by changing who he is entirely before going to these areas.

4) Jekyll also sets up a house for Hyde in <u>Soho</u>, and furnishes it in "<u>luxury and good taste</u>". This <u>ties</u> him, a respectable gentleman, to a disreputable part of the city.

KEY QUOTE

"Soho...with its muddy ways, and slatternly passengers"

Although they'd insist otherwise, some Victorian gents were quite familiar with the dodgy parts of town. Dark alleys, narrow streets and constant fog — the perfect place for hiding your secret night-time exploits.

Section One — Background and Context

Victorian Religion and Science

The Victorians were a very religious lot, but they were also really keen on their science.
You probably don't need me to tell you that these two don't always play nicely together...

Victorian society was very religious

A family Bible reading

1) <u>Christianity</u> had a <u>strong influence</u> on many areas of everyday life in Victorian England. One particularly influential <u>branch</u> of Christianity was called <u>Evangelicalism</u>.

2) The Evangelicals taught that <u>all</u> people are <u>naturally sinful</u>, and that it's up to individuals to <u>seek forgiveness</u> from <u>God</u>. They should do this by living according to a strict <u>moral</u> and <u>religious code</u> — with an emphasis on <u>total morality</u> and avoiding <u>sin</u>.

Character — Jekyll

Jekyll is <u>particularly critical</u> of his own sinfulness, more so than any other character. He thinks of sin as "the <u>doom</u> and <u>burden</u> of our life". He creates Hyde in an attempt to <u>rid</u> himself of this "extraneous evil".

Darwin's theory of evolution was controversial

1) In the early 1800s, Christianity taught that <u>God</u> created every species to be <u>perfectly adapted</u> to its environment. The Book of Genesis also taught that humans were made in <u>God's image</u>, different from all <u>other animals</u> and ruling over them.

2) In contrast, <u>some scientists</u> argued that species <u>evolved</u> (developed) gradually over time. There were many different theories of how this process occurred.

3) <u>Darwin</u> put forward his theory in 'On the Origin of Species', published in <u>1859</u>. Darwin's book claimed that all creatures evolved from common ancestors through a process called 'natural selection'. In a later book, he wrote about <u>humans</u>, arguing that they shared a <u>common ancestor</u> with <u>apes</u>.

4) Darwin's writings went <u>against</u> the Christian idea that man's nature was <u>different</u> from other animals. It's an <u>unsettling</u> idea that there may be an <u>animalistic side</u> to everyone, capable of <u>uncivilised</u> acts and <u>violent</u> crimes.

A satire of Darwin's ideas from 1861

Stevenson uses this idea in the novel. Hyde is described as the "<u>animal within</u>" Henry Jekyll. He "<u>seems hardly human</u>", lets out a scream of "<u>animal terror</u>" and Poole says he is "<u>like a monkey</u>". Hyde is also <u>shorter</u> than Jekyll, which could suggest that he's a <u>less evolved</u> version of the doctor.

Show how context is linked to the events in the novel...

Science and religion can be tricky topics, but the thing to focus on is how they might've influenced Stevenson's writing. It's good to mention the bits of the novel that are particularly frightening for Victorians.

Practice Questions

Here's a page of questions on historical context — the perfect way to make sure you've taken in all the juicy facts in this section. Quick Questions only need a sentence or less, but aim for a paragraph for the In-depth ones.

Quick Questions

1) Which monarch was on the throne when *Jekyll and Hyde* was published?

2) Give one reason why a man would want to be a gentleman.

3) Which of the following statements about Victorian gentlemen is NOT true?
   a) They were vulnerable to blackmail.
   b) They did not care about their appearance.
   c) They were obsessed with their reputations.

4) Give two examples of problems with slum housing in London.

5) Why did Victorian London suffer from smoke?

6) a) Which branch of Christianity particularly influenced Victorian life?
   b) Which of these is one of its teachings?
      i) Some human beings are naturally sinful.
      ii) Most human beings are naturally sinful.
      iii) All human beings are naturally sinful.

7) a) What was the name of Darwin's famous book on evolutionary theory?
   b) In what year was it first published?

In-depth Questions

1) In the first chapter of the novel, how does Stevenson show that Gabriel Utterson is a gentleman?

2) Give an example from the novel and explain how it shows that reputation is important to the following characters:
   a) Mr Enfield
   b) Dr Lanyon

3) What evidence is there in *Jekyll and Hyde* that society in Victorian England was religious?

4) Using what you know about the period, why might Hyde be particularly frightening for Victorian readers?

Analysis — Story of the Door

A door? Which door, I hear you ask. Why, the one Hyde goes into after calmly trampling a child, of course...

You meet the odd couple of Mr Utterson and Mr Enfield

1) This chapter introduces Gabriel <u>Utterson</u>, a well-respected lawyer.

2) Utterson and <u>Enfield</u>, his distant relation, appear to have <u>nothing in common</u>, but they <u>enjoy</u> spending time together.

3) The two men go on Sunday walks together during which they say "nothing". Their <u>silence</u> creates <u>suspense</u> and a <u>lack of information</u>.

> **Character — Utterson**
>
> Utterson is a <u>typical Victorian gentleman</u>. He's "embarrassed" in conversations and <u>hides</u> his <u>emotions</u>. He's <u>rational</u> — as a lawyer he deals in <u>facts</u> and <u>evidence</u>.

> **Theme — Secrecy**
>
> In Victorian society, <u>discretion</u> was preferred to <u>gossip</u>. It's Enfield's rule to <u>not ask questions</u> if something seems <u>suspicious</u> — he doesn't want to know about <u>immoral</u> behaviour. In <u>contrast</u>, Utterson is often "the last reputable acquaintance" of men who have ruined their reputation, which suggests that he's more <u>tolerant</u> of the <u>sins</u> of others.

They set the scene for the start of the mystery

1) Utterson and Enfield walk down a <u>prosperous</u> street in London. This is shown by the condition of the houses, which have "<u>freshly painted</u> shutters" and "<u>well-polished</u> brasses".

2) One building with "<u>nothing but a door</u>" contrasts with the other buildings on the <u>clean</u>, <u>smart</u> street. Stevenson uses <u>negative adjectives</u> such as "sinister" and "sordid" to make it stand out as <u>unusual</u> from its surroundings.

3) Later in the chapter we're told that Mr Hyde has a <u>key</u> to the building and has been <u>inside</u>. This link is <u>important</u> — Hyde and the building are both <u>sinister</u> and <u>disturbing</u>.

© Nick Collinge @ Love It Studios

Enfield's story introduces Mr Hyde

> **Theme — Reputation**
>
> <u>Reputation</u> was <u>important</u> among <u>upper</u> and <u>middle-class</u> Victorians — Utterson and Enfield promise not to <u>discuss</u> Hyde, whose cheque is signed by Jekyll, in order to <u>protect</u> Jekyll's reputation.

1) Enfield tells Utterson that he saw Hyde <u>trample</u> a young girl. Enfield's <u>language</u> emphasises how <u>evil</u> Hyde is — he describes him as "like <u>Satan</u>".

2) The way Hyde tramples "<u>calmly</u>" over the little girl shows how <u>easily</u> he does <u>violent</u> things. When he produces a cheque signed by a man whose name Enfield <u>won't mention</u>, this creates <u>mystery</u>.

3) Enfield <u>can't</u> put his finger on why Hyde makes him feel so <u>uncomfortable</u>. He says, "I never saw a man I so disliked, and yet I scarce know why." This hints at an <u>unusual evil</u> within Hyde.

"Let us make a bargain never to refer to this again"

In this opening chapter a strange story is told and a strange man is introduced, but a vow is made never to talk about it again. It'd be annoying if the novel ended there, but luckily for you the mystery continues...

Analysis — Search for Mr Hyde

Utterson decides to play detective to find the child trampler. He's no Sherlock Holmes, let's put it that way.

Henry Jekyll's will is mysterious

Theme — Science

Jekyll is interested in the "fanciful" side of science, whereas Lanyon is a more traditional scientist.

1) Utterson has Jekyll's <u>will</u>, which says that if Jekyll <u>dies</u> or <u>disappears</u>, all his things should go to <u>Edward Hyde</u>. Utterson <u>suspects</u> that Hyde is <u>blackmailing</u> Jekyll.

2) When Utterson visits Dr <u>Lanyon</u>, he discovers that Lanyon and Jekyll <u>fell out</u> over Jekyll's <u>scientific</u> work, which Lanyon describes as "<u>unscientific balderdash</u>". This hints that Jekyll's experiments are taking a <u>darker</u> direction than <u>conventional</u> science.

3) Utterson leaves <u>none the wiser</u> about <u>who</u> Hyde is and <u>why</u> Jekyll is so <u>interested</u> in him:

- This <u>lack of information</u> about Hyde leaves Utterson feeling <u>unsettled</u>. He dreams that he's "<u>haunted</u>" by a man who has <u>no face</u>, who appears on every street of an almost <u>nightmarish</u> version of London.

- These dreams show that Hyde is affecting Utterson's <u>subconscious</u> and leaves him wanting to <u>see</u> Hyde's face so that "<u>the mystery would lighten</u>" — visual <u>evidence</u> is important to the <u>rational</u> Utterson.

Utterson meets Hyde and feels unsettled

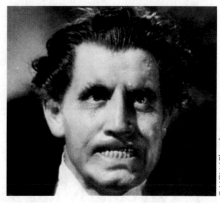

1) Utterson begins to "haunt" the <u>door</u> where Enfield first saw Hyde. It's <u>night-time</u> and the street is "<u>solitary</u>" and "<u>silent</u>" before Hyde appears — this creates a sense of <u>expectation</u>.

2) This is the first time we meet Hyde properly — he's described as "<u>pale and dwarfish</u>" with a "<u>savage laugh</u>". Utterson emphasises that Hyde seems "<u>hardly human</u>" — this hints that he's <u>less evolved</u>. Like Enfield, Utterson <u>can't explain</u> what makes Hyde so <u>unsettling</u>.

3) When Utterson implies that Jekyll told him about Hyde, Hyde <u>strongly denies</u> it. The reader is left to <u>wonder</u> how he could be <u>so certain</u>.

© MGM / Photofest

Jekyll's house is an important symbol

1) Utterson <u>knew all along</u> that the building Hyde went into is a laboratory that's attached to Jekyll's house, but the reader only finds this out <u>now</u>. The way information is given out <u>bit by bit</u> adds to the <u>mystery</u>.

Writer's Techniques — Symbolism

Jekyll's "<u>comfortable</u>" house <u>contrasts</u> with the "<u>sinister</u>" laboratory that Hyde goes into. These buildings are <u>physically connected</u>, which symbolises that Jekyll and Hyde are <u>two different sides</u> of the <u>same</u> person.

2) Jekyll's <u>house</u> has "a great air of wealth and comfort", which symbolises his <u>respectable</u> nature and <u>successful</u> life.

3) When Jekyll's butler Poole tells Utterson that the servants all have orders to obey Hyde, Utterson is more <u>convinced</u> than ever that Jekyll is being made to <u>pay</u> for "some old <u>sin</u>". This explanation shows Utterson's <u>concern</u> for Jekyll's <u>reputation</u>.

KEY QUOTE

"There is something more, if I could find a name for it"

Utterson manages to collar Hyde but he scarpers before Utterson even has the chance to say "Oi, that's not gentlemanly behaviour now, is it". Hyde makes Utterson feel uneasy, but he can't put his finger on why.

Analysis — Dr Jekyll was Quite at Ease

Utterson finally pins down Jekyll. Time for some tough lawyer-ish interrogation you'd think. Not quite...

Jekyll is a popular, respectable man

1) Two weeks later, Jekyll invites Utterson and some other "intelligent, <u>reputable</u>" upper-class men to one of his dinner parties. This reflects the <u>social circle</u> that Jekyll moves in.

2) This is the <u>first time</u> the reader meets Jekyll. His dinner parties show that he's a <u>sociable</u> man who fits in with <u>respectable</u> Victorian upper-class society.

3) Jekyll is described as a <u>kind</u> man. However, he also has a "<u>slyish cast</u>" — this hints that he's hiding something or has a <u>darker side</u> to his personality.

© Photos 12 / Alamy

Utterson tries to talk to Jekyll about his will

Background and Context

Lanyon thinks Jekyll is spending time on "scientific <u>heresies</u>" (Lanyon thinks that Jekyll's scientific work goes <u>against</u> God). The 1800s were a time of scientific <u>progress</u> — but some of these discoveries raised questions about the <u>dangers</u> of scientific discoveries.

1) Utterson questions Jekyll about the will. He treats the mystery as a <u>case</u> that can be solved <u>rationally</u>.

2) Jekyll tries to <u>hide</u> the fact that he doesn't want to discuss it and <u>changes the subject</u> to talk about Lanyon. This makes the reader <u>curious</u> about why he can't even tell his close friend and lawyer what's going on.

3) Jekyll sees Lanyon as "ignorant" because he <u>dismisses</u> his work. This suggests that Jekyll is so <u>determined</u> to pursue his "fanciful" experiments, that he'll <u>risk</u> losing friends over it.

Jekyll clearly has something to hide

1) Jekyll does all he can to avoid explaining the will:

- Jekyll says that he's in a <u>strange</u> situation that "cannot be mended by <u>talking</u>". This <u>secrecy</u> builds <u>suspense</u>.

- He also tells Utterson that he has "<u>a very great interest</u>" in Hyde — but again, he <u>won't explain</u> why.

- Jekyll claims that "the moment I <u>choose</u>, I can be <u>rid</u> of Mr Hyde", but we find out later that this <u>isn't true</u>.

Theme — Secrecy

Victorians <u>hid</u> what they saw as their <u>immoral desires</u> to maintain <u>respectability</u>. Jekyll <u>hides the truth</u> about Hyde from Utterson because Hyde is the <u>immoral</u> side of his character.

2) Utterson tries to get Jekyll <u>out of trouble</u>. He's <u>more interested</u> in <u>preserving</u> Jekyll's <u>reputation</u> than in the <u>morality</u> of what Jekyll might have done — like a true Victorian gentleman, he'd rather <u>not know</u> the details of Jekyll's <u>sins</u>, so he doesn't press him for answers about Hyde.

Mention the early signs of Jekyll's dual personality...

It'll impress the examiner if you can talk about the less obvious evidence for Jekyll's double personality. He seems like a pleasant, sociable guy, but he's got a "slyish" look, which hints that he's got a dark side.

Analysis — The Carew Murder Case

Hyde moves on from trampling kids to beating old men to death. He sounds quite the upstanding citizen.

Hyde murders Danvers Carew

1) This chapter begins <u>nearly a year later</u>. The maid's account of Carew's murder is written like a <u>police statement</u>. This <u>distances</u> the reader from the event itself. We're also <u>limited</u> to the maid's <u>perspective</u> — she's "romantically given" so it's hard to know how much we can <u>believe</u>.

2) The maid's description of the murder of Carew is a <u>shocking</u> change of tone in her initially <u>peaceful</u> account. The fact that she faints shows how <u>shocking</u> the murder was.

© Nick Collinge @ Love It Studios

3) The old man appears <u>polite</u> and full of "old-world <u>kindness</u>". This emphasises his <u>innocence</u> and shows how <u>evil</u> Hyde is — he attacks Carew for <u>no reason</u>.

4) Hyde is described as trampling Carew with "<u>ape-like fury</u>". This animalistic description shows how he's <u>primal</u> and <u>savage</u>.

Writer's Techniques — Language

Stevenson appeals to the readers sense of <u>hearing</u> as well as sight by describing how Carew's bones were "<u>audibly</u>" shattered. This makes the attack even more <u>horrific</u> and <u>vivid</u> as you <u>imagine</u> how <u>terrible</u> it would be to <u>hear</u> someone's bones breaking.

5) A lot of <u>gruesome</u> detail is given — Hyde "<u>clubbed</u>" Carew, "<u>trampling</u>" him and giving him a "<u>storm of blows</u>" so that his body "<u>jumped</u> upon the roadway".

6) Hyde leaves Carew "<u>incredibly mangled</u>" on the street — it's a <u>brutal</u> and <u>shocking</u> crime.

Utterson and the police search for Hyde

1) The policeman's reaction to the identification of Carew as the victim shows that <u>everyone</u> has a <u>double nature</u> — he's initially <u>concerned</u>, but soon "professional <u>ambition</u>" to turn the situation to his advantage takes over. Stevenson shows that <u>hypocrisy</u> is <u>widespread</u> in Victorian society.

2) Utterson leads the police to Hyde's house. Hyde lives down a "<u>dingy</u> street" in a "<u>dismal</u> quarter of Soho". Utterson sees it as "some city in a <u>nightmare</u>" — it's a place of <u>darkness</u> and swirling <u>fog</u> which makes him feel <u>uneasy</u>. This <u>contrasts</u> with the comfortable house and <u>respectable</u> area that Jekyll lives in.

Writer's Techniques — Setting

Soho was an area associated with <u>poverty</u> and <u>immorality</u>. It's located in the <u>richer</u>, more <u>respectable</u> West End of London. This reflects the <u>relationship</u> between Jekyll and Hyde — the <u>immoral</u> <u>Hyde</u> is located <u>within</u> the <u>respectable Jekyll</u>.

Theme — Dual Nature of Man

Stevenson uses the minor character of Hyde's landlady to develop the idea that it's <u>human nature</u> to <u>conceal</u> our <u>faults</u> — she has an "<u>evil</u> face, smoothed by <u>hypocrisy</u>" but "her <u>manners</u> were <u>excellent</u>", which shows that she's putting on a front of respectability.

Comment on the symbolism of the settings...

Show the examiner that you understand that Stevenson uses settings as symbols for the characters in the novel. Jekyll's house is another great example — it looks respectable, but it's connected to the sinister lab.

Analysis — Incident of the Letter

Now it's Henry Jekyll's time to have a funny turn. But one that's a little more sickly and a little less violent.

Jekyll acts strangely after Carew's murder

When Utterson visits Jekyll, he finds him behaving oddly:

- Jekyll is in his laboratory when Utterson goes to see him, which is unusual because Utterson hasn't visited his friend there before. This is the "dingy" building we associate with Hyde, and Utterson feels a "sense of strangeness" when he goes in which creates tension and unease.

- Jekyll looks "sick" and speaks in a "feverish manner" — this shows how agitated he is about the murder. He's determined to be rid of Hyde, swearing to God that he'll never see him again.

- But he's still holding back information. He says he has "grounds for certainty" that Hyde will not return, but he "cannot share" with anyone what these are. This increases the mystery.

Stevenson includes letters in his narrative

Writer's Techniques — Structure and Narrative

The reader learns a lot through letters and documents. These make the gradual unravelling events of the story seem more realistic. See p. 42-43 for more on this.

1) Jekyll claims that he's received a letter from Hyde, which he gives to Utterson because he's worried it will affect his reputation. Utterson is relieved — he was concerned that Jekyll's name would be dragged into a scandal.

2) Initially Utterson is convinced by the letter's authenticity, but when Poole says that nothing was delivered, he starts to doubt it. This shows that even written documents can't be trusted. Stevenson gives the reader reasons throughout the novel to doubt what we're told — it creates an atmosphere of intrigue.

Utterson leaps to the wrong conclusion

1) Utterson takes the letter home and shows it to Guest, his head clerk. It's Guest who realises that Hyde's writing looks very similar to Jekyll's.

2) Utterson "struggled" with himself before asking Guest for more information. This makes it seem as if Utterson is reluctant to uncover what might be an unpleasant truth.

3) Utterson warns Guest not to speak about the letter — this adds another layer of secrecy to the case. Utterson comes to the conclusion that Jekyll has forged the note for Hyde.

Theme — Secrecy

Utterson usually keeps problems to himself. Even when he asks for Guest's help, he does it indirectly, rather than being upfront. It's all part of the Victorian code of restraint and concealing emotions.

© Nick Collinge @ Love It Studios

KEY QUOTE

"If it came to a trial, your name might appear"

Utterson reckons that Jekyll is protecting Hyde, but he's not too fussed about it — he's just worried that Jekyll's good name will be ruined. Reputation over justice, eh? That's Victorian gentlemen for you...

Analysis — Remarkable Incident of Dr Lanyon

Things really do start taking a turn for the strange and mysterious now. Well, even more of a turn than before.

Jekyll seems to be back to normal — but not for long

1) Time passes and it's as though Hyde "never existed". This is ironic because Hyde does exist — but only within Jekyll, who is currently the model of Victorian respectability.

2) A "new life" begins for Jekyll. He holds dinner parties with Utterson and Lanyon, where he acts like he did in the old days. He does good deeds and is "at peace".

3) However, after two months Jekyll suddenly retreats from society once again without explanation. Jekyll's odd behaviour adds to the atmosphere of mystery.

© Nick Collinge @ Love It Studios

The sudden change in Lanyon is shocking

Utterson visits Lanyon to see if he knows more and is "shocked" by the change he finds in him:

- Lanyon appears older and balder, but most importantly he seems to have a "deep-seated terror of the mind". This extreme change shows how profoundly affected he is by what he's seen. The reader doesn't find out what's happened which causes the suspense to build.

- Lanyon believes he'll die soon and says that "if we knew all, we should be more glad to get away." Lanyon's use of language shows how much he's changed — the first time we meet Lanyon he's an articulate man of science, but now his speech is vague and cryptic.

Utterson's honour prevents him from discovering the truth

Theme — Dual Nature of Man

Jekyll writes in his reply to Utterson that "I am the chief of sinners, I am the chief of sufferers also." This hints at the internal conflict between Jekyll and Hyde and suggests that the more Hyde sins, the more Jekyll suffers.

1) Utterson writes to Jekyll asking why Lanyon feels so negatively about him. Jekyll's reply is "darkly mysterious", telling Utterson, "You must suffer me to go my own dark way." This hints that Jekyll's involved in a dangerous situation.

2) A fortnight later Lanyon dies and leaves Utterson an envelope. If he reads it he'll find out the truth, but another envelope inside says it can't be opened till the death or disappearance of Jekyll.

3) Utterson is tempted to open the letter but he's a man of "professional honour", so he locks it in his safe. This shows that Utterson values moral principles above personal curiosity.

Writer's Techniques — Symbolism

The locked safe could also symbolise Utterson's unwillingness to confront the mystery — he'd rather lock it away.

KEY QUOTE

"the packet slept in the inmost corner of his private safe"

The situation makes no sense. But what's this, a letter explaining everything? Best lock it away then."
Dangling letter-shaped carrots in front of us like this is mean — Stevenson sure knows how to tease.

Analysis — Incident at the Window & The Last Night

Jekyll seems to be in some big trouble here. Is it murder? Some weird disease? Erm. Not quite.

Jekyll's secret is nearly revealed

1) Jekyll talks to Utterson and Enfield from the <u>window</u> of his <u>laboratory</u>. As they <u>talk</u>, a look of "abject <u>terror</u> and <u>despair</u>" comes across <u>Jekyll's face</u> — it's a sign that he's about to <u>transform</u> into <u>Hyde</u>.

2) The look on Jekyll's face "<u>froze</u> the very <u>blood</u>" of Utterson and Enfield. They <u>don't know</u> the truth about Jekyll and Hyde at this point — but their <u>reaction</u> shows that they <u>feel</u> they've witnessed something <u>strange</u> and <u>inexplicable</u>.

Writer's Techniques — Gothic Novel

This hints at the dark or possibly <u>supernatural forces</u> that are acting on <u>Jekyll</u>. <u>Supernatural</u> or <u>unexplained</u> events are an <u>important</u> feature of the <u>Gothic</u> novel.

Poole is clearly concerned about Jekyll

Jekyll locks himself in his cabinet — a small room in his laboratory.

Utterson gets a surprise visit from Poole, who's <u>worried</u> about Jekyll's irrational behaviour:

- Poole <u>avoids</u> Utterson's questions. Utterson tells him to "be explicit" but Poole <u>won't say</u> what's happened. This <u>lack</u> of information <u>increases suspense</u>.

- Poole openly admits that he's <u>afraid</u> — by admitting his <u>emotions</u> (rather than <u>hiding</u> them), he makes Utterson realise how <u>serious</u> the situation is.

- Poole's fear makes Utterson feel "<u>frightened</u>", which then "<u>irritated</u>" him — he's a <u>rational</u> person who's more comfortable dealing with <u>facts</u> than <u>emotions</u>.

© Nick Collinge @ Love It Studios

The terrified servants increase the suspense

1) When Utterson and Poole arrive at Jekyll's house, one of the maids is "<u>hysterical</u>" with fear. Utterson thinks this behaviour is "Very <u>irregular</u>, very <u>unseemly</u>" — he's still <u>concerned</u> with the <u>appearance</u> of <u>order</u>.

2) Utterson finds out what has been making Poole so <u>anxious</u>:

Poole has heard <u>crying</u> from inside the cabinet. He was given a <u>desperate</u> note for the chemist saying "<u>For God's sake</u>...find me some of the old".

Jekyll's <u>desperation</u> is clear from the <u>anxious tone</u> of his letter. There's <u>mystery</u> about why he needs the medicine <u>so badly</u>.

The door to the cabinet remains <u>locked</u> — meals are left outside and taken when "<u>nobody was looking</u>."

The <u>locked door</u> is another <u>barrier</u> to revealing Jekyll's secret. There's a sense that something <u>disturbing</u> and <u>dangerous</u> is <u>hidden</u> behind it.

Poole saw someone outside the cabinet — if it was Jekyll, it looked like he was wearing a <u>mask</u>.

The <u>mask</u> is an <u>important image</u>. It explores the idea of <u>dual personality</u> — <u>Hyde</u> is a <u>disguise</u> which allows Jekyll to commit <u>immoral</u> acts <u>without ruining</u> his respectable <u>reputation</u>.

Analysis — The Last Night (continued)

Utterson struggles to find a rational explanation

Poole and Utterson have <u>different explanations</u> for what's been going on:

- Poole is <u>convinced</u> that Jekyll has been <u>murdered</u> by Hyde, who's still in the cabinet. He's sure it's Hyde because of the man's <u>appearance</u> and the sense of <u>unease</u> he felt around him.

- Utterson thinks that Poole's explanation is a "<u>wild</u>" tale that doesn't hold up to <u>reason</u>. He believes that Jekyll has an <u>illness</u> which has changed his appearance and caused him to withdraw from society. This shows that Utterson is still looking for a <u>rational</u> explanation.

Utterson decides to break the door down...

1) Poole <u>convinces</u> Utterson that Hyde murdered Jekyll and that he's still in the cabinet with his victim. Poole says that his explanation is based on "<u>feelings</u>", not "<u>evidence</u>", but feels <u>convinced</u> by it. This highlights the lack of <u>reliable evidence</u> available to Utterson.

2) Despite his anxiety, Utterson approaches breaking down the door in a typically <u>logical</u> way — he delivers orders and tries to calm the servant's nerves.

> **Writer's Techniques — Structure**
>
> This scene is <u>climactic</u> — when the door is broken down, the mystery will be <u>revealed</u>.

© United Archives GmbH / Alamy

3) The locked door <u>symbolises</u> the <u>barriers</u> to finding and accepting the <u>truth</u> of man's <u>dual nature</u>. Utterson and Poole are "<u>appalled</u>" that they've broken in to Jekyll's cabinet — this act goes <u>against</u> their usual <u>restraint</u>. They are reluctant to <u>disrupt</u> the <u>order</u> of their <u>civilised</u> world.

...and finds Hyde dead on the floor inside

1) Utterson and Poole find Hyde's "<u>sorely contorted</u>" body inside the cabinet — but <u>Jekyll</u> is <u>nowhere</u> to be found. The "crushed phial" in Hyde's hand shows that he's <u>committed suicide</u>.

2) The glowing fire and cosy room <u>contrast</u> with the <u>horrible</u> discovery of <u>Hyde's body</u> — this highlights the <u>horror</u> of what's happened to Jekyll's <u>ordered</u> existence.

3) The "<u>commonplace</u>" room shows that Jekyll was just an <u>ordinary</u> person — this emphasises that <u>his concerns</u> about the <u>good</u> and <u>bad</u> within him are <u>relevant to everyone</u>.

> **Character — Hyde**
>
> Utterson sees "<u>blasphemies</u>" written on one of Jekyll's favourite <u>religious</u> texts. This shows how Hyde takes <u>pleasure</u> in <u>undermining</u> the <u>good</u> side of Jekyll's personality.

4) Utterson finds a <u>letter</u> from Jekyll which he goes home to <u>read</u> with <u>Lanyon's account</u>. We're told "this mystery was now to be <u>explained</u>."

Write about how Stevenson creates suspense...

Show you understand Stevenson's techniques by commenting on how he builds suspense. This chapter, and the novel as a whole, is packed full of it — the scared servants, Poole's anxiety and the locked door.

Analysis — Dr Lanyon's Narrative

Right folks, it's story time with Lanyon. I'd hide behind the sofa — a horrifying bombshell is coming our way.

Lanyon narrative is a flash-back

1) Lanyon's letter takes the reader back to the <u>middle</u> of the main narrative. This <u>shifting</u> narrative makes the story feel quite <u>fragmented</u>, as if the truth is only being revealed in <u>parts</u>.

2) <u>Before</u> Jekyll shut himself away, he sent a letter asking <u>Lanyon</u> to force open his <u>cabinet</u> and take one of the <u>drawers</u>. It's a <u>strange</u> request.

3) The "<u>blood-red</u>" colour of the chemicals in the drawer hint at the <u>sinister</u> and <u>mysterious</u> nature of Jekyll's experiments. Even Lanyon (a fellow scientist) can "make <u>no guess</u>" at what some of the chemicals are, which shows how far Jekyll has <u>strayed</u> from traditional science.

> **Writer's Techniques — Narrative**
>
> In this chapter, we <u>finally</u> hear what scared Lanyon to death back in Chapter 6. The <u>first-person</u> narrative makes the events seem more <u>believable</u>.

Lanyon meets Hyde for the first time

© MGM / Photofest

1) When the messenger arrives, Lanyon <u>doesn't know</u> that it's <u>Hyde</u>, although the reader does. This creates <u>tension</u> — we know what he's capable of.

2) Hyde arrives at midnight — Stevenson frequently <u>links</u> Hyde with the <u>night</u> to emphasise his link with <u>secret</u> deeds and <u>hidden</u> desires.

3) Lanyon also experiences the <u>odd</u> feeling that other characters have around Hyde. Lanyon thought this was just "<u>personal distaste</u>", but later <u>realises</u> it's caused by something "much deeper in the <u>nature of man</u>".

> **Theme — Dual Nature of Man**
>
> Meeting Hyde causes Lanyon to <u>confront</u> an <u>unpleasant truth</u> about <u>human nature</u> — that <u>everyone</u> has evil inside them.

Lanyon's curiosity leads him to discover Jekyll's secret

 KEY EVENT

> **Theme — Science and Religion**
>
> Hyde says that if Lanyon sees Jekyll's discovery, it would open "new avenues to <u>fame</u> and <u>power</u>", but it would also "<u>stagger</u> the unbelief of <u>Satan</u>". This shows how knowledge which challenges God's order is both <u>attractive</u> and <u>dangerous</u>.

1) Hyde asks Lanyon if the "<u>greed of curiosity</u>" has got the better of him and offers to let Lanyon <u>watch</u> him take the potion. Lanyon then <u>sees</u> Hyde <u>transform</u> into Jekyll.

2) Stevenson describes the transformation <u>vividly</u> — Hyde's face became "suddenly black". This detail emphasises how <u>distressing</u> it would be to witness.

3) After seeing the transformation, Lanyon says that his "life is <u>shaken</u> to its roots". Everything he believes in has been <u>shattered</u> — Jekyll has <u>proven</u> to Lanyon that the type of science he <u>denied</u> is <u>real</u>.

4) Although this chapter gives us more information, Stevenson still doesn't explain <u>why</u> the transformation happened. There are some things that <u>only Jekyll</u> can <u>explain</u>, which increases our <u>anticipation</u>.

 KEY QUOTE

"the features seemed to melt"

That was a shocker — Jekyll and Hyde turned out to be the same person. Or not — the story is well known today, so we're not as surprised as the Victorians would have been. It's still a cracking mystery though.

Section Two — Discussion of Chapters

Analysis — Henry Jekyll's Full Statement of the Case

Finally, the whole mystery is revealed. Except what Jekyll put in his potion. Typical, isn't it...

Jekyll talks about his discovery of man's dual nature

Writer's Techniques — Structure

Jekyll's account <u>fills in</u> the <u>mysterious gaps</u> in the novel — he's the only one to actually put into words what he did. Things which were left <u>unexplained</u> start to <u>make sense</u>, such as Jekyll's absences and why Hyde is named in Jekyll's will.

1) As a young man, Jekyll was "<u>fond</u> of the <u>respect</u>" others gave him. His <u>concern</u> with how others <u>viewed</u> him led him to "<u>wear</u>" a more <u>serious appearance</u> than he actually <u>felt</u> — this is the Victorian <u>ideal</u> of a <u>respectable</u> gentleman.

2) At the same time, he was <u>tempted</u> by "<u>pleasures</u>" which he felt <u>guilty</u> about — he thought they would <u>affect</u> his <u>reputation</u> so he "<u>concealed</u>" them.

3) Jekyll explains that he wanted to <u>hide</u> his sins because he set such <u>high standards</u> for himself — he claims that it's not because his desires were particularly <u>awful</u>. This makes us <u>sympathise</u> with Jekyll — in <u>understanding</u> his motivation, we can see how <u>stressful</u> he found the strain of being <u>respectable</u>.

He wanted to enjoy his bad side without feeling shame

© Nick Collinge @ Love It Studios

1) Jekyll dreamt of <u>separating</u> his <u>good</u> and <u>bad</u> sides — his bad side could be <u>immoral</u> without feeling <u>held back</u> by the need to be <u>respectable</u>, and the good side wouldn't feel <u>guilty</u> about his <u>desires</u> to do immoral things.

2) He says it would be a "<u>miracle</u>" to make his "beloved <u>daydream</u>" a reality — this language suggests that he knows that his plan is <u>impossible</u>, yet Jekyll is <u>desperate</u> to find a solution to his guilt and shame.

3) Jekyll used "<u>transcendental</u>" science to separate his two sides. Although he was aware of the <u>risks</u>, the "<u>temptation</u> of a discovery" was <u>too much</u> for him to <u>resist</u> — this shows that knowledge can be both <u>fascinating</u> and <u>dangerous</u>.

4) As Hyde, he feels <u>younger</u> and more <u>carefree</u>, but also <u>more wicked</u>. Despite Hyde's evil, Jekyll feels a "leap of <u>welcome</u>" for <u>Hyde</u> — this shows how <u>tempting</u> it can be to indulge your darker side.

The experiment doesn't go to plan

1) Jekyll says that if he had approached the experiment with <u>good intentions</u>, he could have created an "angel". However, during the experiment, he was motivated by his <u>desire</u> to do <u>sinful</u> things without <u>repercussions</u>. This resulted in the <u>purely evil</u> Hyde while Jekyll remained a <u>mixture</u> of good and evil.

2) Jekyll initially wants to use Hyde to <u>indulge</u> his "undignified" <u>pleasures</u> but in the hands of Hyde, these become "<u>monstrous</u>". Hyde's sins are <u>worse</u> because he's so <u>evil</u> — there's no good in him to <u>balance</u> his behaviour.

Theme — Secrecy

Jekyll <u>doesn't tell</u> us what immoral activities Hyde got up to. This increases the <u>horror</u> because it's left to the reader's <u>imagination</u>.

3) Jekyll is <u>shocked</u> by the extent of Hyde's evil but at this stage <u>justifies</u> it by believing that it's "<u>Hyde alone</u>" who is <u>guilty</u>. Jekyll doesn't see Hyde's actions as his actions — this is <u>hypocritical</u>.

Analysis — Henry Jekyll's Full Statement of the Case

Jekyll starts to lose control

The <u>two sides</u> of Jekyll <u>struggle</u> with each other:

- One morning Jekyll wakes up to find that he's turned into Hyde <u>without</u> taking any drugs. Hyde has grown <u>taller</u> as his evil personality has been more "<u>nourished</u>".

- Jekyll <u>decides</u> to stop taking the potion that turns him into Hyde and for two months leads a good, <u>respectable</u> life. However, he is soon "tortured with <u>throes</u> and <u>longings</u>" to be <u>Hyde</u> again.

- Jekyll gives in to <u>temptation</u> and takes the potion. That night, he <u>brutally murders</u> Carew. This shows that he's <u>losing control</u>.

Theme — Dual Nature of Man

This suggests that the <u>more</u> you <u>repress</u> your desires, the <u>more strongly</u> they will come out in the end — Jekyll kept Hyde "<u>long caged</u>" but he returned <u>more evil</u> than ever.

Theme — Violence

It's <u>shocking</u> how much <u>pleasure</u> Hyde gets from the murder — he feels "<u>glee</u>" and tasted "<u>delight</u> from every blow".

He doesn't want to be Hyde anymore

1) Jekyll is <u>horrified</u> by the murder. He decides to live a <u>respectable</u> life, but <u>returns</u> to his <u>immoral</u> ways as an "<u>ordinary secret sinner</u>" — this phrase reminds us that <u>everyone</u> does bad things and it's the <u>shame</u> Jekyll feels for hiding these sins that <u>motivates</u> him to create Hyde.

2) One day, Jekyll suddenly turns into Hyde while sitting in the park. He believes this happened because he started to <u>sin</u> again <u>as Jekyll</u> — this destroyed the "balance" of his soul.

Character — Jekyll

Jekyll turns into Hyde after feeling <u>satisfied</u> by his own "<u>active goodwill</u>". It's <u>ironic</u> that he transforms into Hyde at a moment when he's congratulating himself on his <u>virtues</u>.

© Nick Collinge @ Love It Studios

3) Jekyll <u>hates</u> "the brute that slept within" him. This shows the <u>hypocritical</u> side of Jekyll — he's <u>struggling</u> to <u>accept</u> that Hyde is part of him.

Jekyll realises his experiment has destroyed his life

1) As Jekyll gets <u>weaker</u>, Hyde gets <u>stronger</u> — this causes <u>tension</u> between the two sides of his character:

- Jekyll now sees Hyde as "<u>inorganic</u>" — something <u>unnatural</u> and <u>artificial</u> that's not part of him.

- Hyde <u>resents</u> the way that Jekyll has turned <u>against</u> him. Hyde begins to play "ape-like tricks" to <u>punish</u> Jekyll.

Theme — Dual Nature of Man

Jekyll's fate is <u>disturbing</u> — especially because the reader is able to <u>apply</u> his thoughts on <u>human nature</u> to their own <u>lives</u>.

2) When Jekyll runs out of a vital ingredient for the potion, there's a sense of <u>approaching horror</u> as the reader <u>knows</u> that Jekyll will be completely <u>taken over</u> by Hyde and his life will be over.

EXAM TIP

Back up your interpretations with evidence...

It will make your essay stand out if you include your own ideas and express a clear opinion. There's no right or wrong answer, as long as you back up your ideas with evidence.

Practice Questions

Just like when Utterson quizzed Jekyll after his dinner party, I'm going to ask some probing questions of my own — but unlike Jekyll it's probably best to answer as well as you can. A few words or a sentence for the Quick Questions and closer to a paragraph for answers to the In-depth Questions would be just dandy.

Quick Questions

1) Briefly explain how Enfield reacts to Hyde's character.

2) Why does Utterson think that Jekyll has put Hyde in his will?

3) How does Jekyll react when Utterson tries to question him about his will?

4) How does Hyde react when Sir Danvers Carew stops to talk to him?

5) Why does Jekyll suddenly shut his window when talking to Utterson and Enfield?

6) Give one example of Jekyll's strange behaviour, which Poole describes to Utterson.

7) Briefly explain what Utterson and Poole find when they break into Jekyll's cabinet.

8) What does Lanyon reveal about the relationship between Jekyll and Hyde in his letter to Utterson?

9) Why does finding out Jekyll's secret result in Lanyon's death?

10) Why does Hyde start to play "ape-like tricks" on Jekyll?

In-depth Questions

1) Briefly explain why the murder of Carew is a key turning point in the novel.

2) Describe the relationship between Jekyll's house and laboratory.

3) Why did Jekyll decide to find a way to split himself in two?

Character Profile — Henry Jekyll & Edward Hyde

Jekyll: a man who has to sin in secret. I feel his pain — I just snuck out of the office for my ninth biscuit.

Dr Henry Jekyll is a pillar of society...

1) Jekyll appears to be a <u>good</u> and <u>respectable</u> man. He's known for his <u>charity</u> work and reads <u>religious</u> texts.

2) He socialises in <u>upper-class</u> circles and holds dinner parties. He's <u>sociable</u> and <u>friendly</u> with "every mark of capacity and <u>kindness</u>".

3) Jekyll <u>behaves</u> in a socially <u>acceptable</u> way — he's very <u>aware</u> of how people see him. He carries his "head high" in public and is "fond of the <u>respect</u>" people give him.

Dr Jekyll is...

Ambitious: "every guarantee of an honourable and distinguished future"

Respectable: "well known and highly considered"

Troubled: "I bring the life of that unhappy Henry Jekyll to an end"

...but he puts on a false face to appear respectable

1) Jekyll has always put on an <u>excessively respectable</u> front — he shows "a more than commonly <u>grave</u> <u>countenance</u> before the public." He <u>worries</u> about his <u>hidden desires</u> — he thinks they're <u>far worse</u> than they are because he's <u>obsessed</u> with appearing <u>respectable</u>.

2) His hidden desires make him feel very <u>guilty</u>, so he creates a "deeper trench" than most people between his good side and his bad side. He <u>hides</u> his desires with an "almost <u>morbid</u> sense of <u>shame</u>."

3) As a result, Jekyll finds himself committed to a "profound <u>duplicity</u> of life", which is why making a potion to split his two sides <u>appeals</u> to him.

Theme — Reputation

Jekyll's <u>excessive</u> sense of guilt for what he sees as his "faults" may be a <u>criticism</u> of the <u>pressures</u> Victorian society placed on people to appear <u>respectable</u>.

"Duplicity" is the act of being deceitful.

© Nick Collinge @ Love It Studios

He is an ambitious man of science

1) Jekyll's experiments in "transcendental medicine" show that he's a <u>brilliant</u> scientist. However, his research is <u>controversial</u> — he's <u>lost</u> the <u>respect</u> of Dr Lanyon because of his "unscientific balderdash".

2) Jekyll's "fanciful" work is not seen as respectable because it crosses the <u>boundary</u> from the science of the <u>material world</u> that Lanyon deals with, into the <u>supernatural</u> and the <u>mystical</u>.

Background and Context — Science

Scientific <u>discoveries</u> in the 1800s sometimes <u>challenged religious beliefs</u>. Jekyll uses science to challenge the religious belief that people should try to lead a life <u>free</u> from <u>sin</u>.

3) By splitting his two sides, Jekyll wants to rid himself of "the <u>curse</u> of <u>mankind</u>" — the curse that man's good and bad sides are <u>bound together</u>. He's motivated by <u>ambition</u> and a <u>selfish</u> desire to be "<u>relieved</u> of all that was <u>unbearable</u>" — a <u>guilty conscience</u>.

4) Jekyll is so <u>desperate</u> to separate his two sides that he willingly "<u>risked death</u>" by drinking the potion he creates. However, instead of splitting his good and bad sides he only succeeds in <u>releasing</u> his bad side. Jekyll remains as <u>divided</u> as he always was — like everyone else, he's made up of good and bad qualities.

Character Profile — Henry Jekyll & Edward Hyde

Edward Hyde embodies wickedness

1) Whereas Jekyll is a <u>mixture</u> of good and evil, Hyde is "<u>pure evil</u>".

2) Hyde seems to be violent for the sake of it — the murder of Carew is an <u>unprovoked</u> and <u>uncontrollable</u> act which he takes "<u>delight</u>" in. It's <u>shocking</u> how much he enjoys violence.

3) His evil is reflected in his <u>appearance</u> — it leaves "an imprint of <u>deformity</u> and <u>decay</u>". Hyde is so evil that it's <u>obvious</u> for everyone to see — there's "something <u>wrong</u> with his appearance".

> **Edward Hyde is...**
>
> **Merciless:** "a man who was without bowels of mercy"
>
> **Strange:** "he gives a strong feeling of deformity"
>
> **Self-centred:** "his every act and thought centred on self"

He's like an animal

Stevenson frequently <u>compares</u> Hyde to <u>animals</u>, particularly apes. This is a comment on <u>people</u> and <u>society</u>:

- The <u>Victorians</u> considered their society to be <u>civilised</u> — they valued propriety, order and self control. They didn't like the idea that people might have a <u>primitive</u>, animalistic side.

- Many Victorians tried to <u>hide</u> what they thought were <u>animalistic desires</u> beneath a <u>civilised</u> <u>exterior</u> — they wanted to appear <u>respectable</u> in order to <u>fit in</u> with civilised society.

- <u>Darwin's theory</u> that man <u>evolved</u> from apes was widely known when the novel was written. Hyde is presented as Jekyll's <u>less evolved</u> side — he's often compared to an <u>ape</u> — and he's <u>smaller</u> and <u>less respectable</u>, which emphasises the idea that the upper-classes were superior.

See p.8 for more on Darwin.

Stevenson's suggestion that there's a <u>primitive</u> Mr Hyde <u>within</u> a <u>respectable</u> man like Dr Jekyll <u>forces</u> the reader to consider that there could be a dark, <u>immoral side</u> to <u>everyone</u>.

He creates strong feelings of hatred and unease

1) People <u>loathe</u> Hyde when they meet him. After Hyde tramples the child, Enfield is shocked that the <u>unemotional</u> doctor looked as though he had a "desire to <u>kill</u>" Hyde. This strong reaction shows that <u>civilised</u> people have <u>immoral</u> thoughts, but don't <u>act</u> on them.

2) Several characters say that they <u>can't explain</u> why they <u>dislike</u> Hyde. The fact that these characters can't (or <u>won't</u>) make any sense of Hyde may reflect the way they've <u>repressed</u> their own <u>dark side</u>.

3) People are <u>disturbed</u> by Hyde's <u>appearance</u> — Enfield says that he is "extraordinary-looking" and Utterson says he can "read Satan's signature" on Hyde's face. His <u>frightening</u> appearance emphasises his <u>difference</u> from other people — he's not quite <u>human</u>.

© MGM / Photofest

"Edward Hyde, alone in the ranks of mankind, was pure evil"

Jekyll fancies indulging his bad side, but Hyde takes sinning to a whole new level. No, not cakes — murder and suchlike. Keep up. It really makes you think about man's capacity for evil.

Character Profile — Henry Jekyll & Edward Hyde

From excitement, to hatred, to death. Jekyll's relationship with Hyde is rocky to say the least...

Jekyll treats Hyde like a separate person...

1) Jekyll creates a completely <u>separate identity</u> for his evil side:

- Jekyll gives his evil side a <u>name</u> — Mr Edward Hyde.

- He furnishes a <u>house</u> and employs a <u>housekeeper</u> for Hyde.

- Jekyll chooses a house in a different part of town and dresses Hyde "very <u>plainly</u>". This makes him seem to be of a <u>lower</u> social class.

2) Jekyll often refers to Hyde in the <u>third person</u> to <u>distance</u> himself from him — for example, "I find it in my heart to pity <u>him</u>".

> **Theme — Dual Nature of Man**
>
> Jekyll <u>alternates</u> between referring to Hyde in the <u>first</u> and <u>third</u> person. This reflects his <u>hypocrisy</u> — he <u>understands</u> that man has a dual nature, but he has <u>trouble accepting</u> that Hyde is part of him. This is clear when he says "He, I say — I cannot say, I".

The first person is when you refer to yourself — "I". The third person is when you refer to someone else — "he".

...but Jekyll and Hyde are two sides of the same coin

1) Jekyll seems in many ways to be the complete <u>opposite</u> of Hyde.

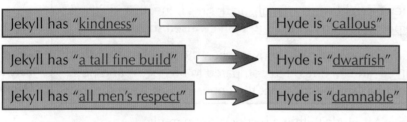

Jekyll has "<u>kindness</u>" → Hyde is "<u>callous</u>"

Jekyll has "<u>a tall fine build</u>" → Hyde is "<u>dwarfish</u>"

Jekyll has "<u>all men's respect</u>" → Hyde is "<u>damnable</u>"

© Nick Collinge @ Love It Studios

2) But they're <u>two sides</u> of the <u>same</u> man:

- Jekyll's <u>obsession</u> with <u>reputation</u> is reflected in Hyde — when Enfield and others threaten to make a "<u>scandal</u>" out of Hyde trampling the child, Hyde says that "No <u>gentleman</u> but wishes to <u>avoid a scene</u>". Hyde has no reputation to protect, but this suggests he's <u>thinking</u> like Jekyll.

- Hyde is "<u>astute</u>" — he's <u>quick-witted</u>. He works out how to get to his drugs when Jekyll turns into Hyde in the park — he isn't just animalistic and primitive, he's <u>intelligent</u> like Jekyll.

Jekyll increasingly loses control of Hyde

1) <u>At first</u>, Jekyll seems to be <u>in control</u> of his immoral side. However, one morning he <u>wakes up as Hyde</u> without taking the drug and says that he's "slowly <u>losing hold</u> of my original and better self".

2) Jekyll becomes increasingly <u>addicted</u> to the immoral side of his personality. He compares himself to a "<u>drunkard</u>" and even though he <u>tries</u> to stop taking the potion that turns him into Hyde, he doesn't give up the <u>house</u> in Soho. This shows how <u>tempting</u> his evil side is.

> **Background and Context**
>
> Victorians <u>repressed</u> their desires in order to maintain <u>respectability</u>. Stevenson may be criticising the <u>dangers</u> of this kind of repression.

3) Jekyll <u>fights</u> to <u>control</u> Hyde, but Hyde just comes out <u>stronger</u> — for example, Hyde <u>murders</u> Carew after Jekyll goes for two months without turning into Hyde.

4) Finally, Jekyll loses control <u>completely</u>, which could suggest that <u>evil</u> is the <u>stronger side</u> of our <u>personality</u>.

Character Profile — Henry Jekyll & Edward Hyde

The hatred between Jekyll and Hyde increases

1) From the beginning, Hyde <u>doesn't care</u> about Jekyll. Hyde just sees Jekyll as a place to <u>conceal</u> himself.

Writer's Techniques — Language

Hyde has "more than a <u>son's indifference</u>", while Jekyll has "more than a <u>father's interest</u>". This father-son terminology suggests that, as Hyde's creator, Jekyll <u>cares</u> about Hyde — however, in the end Hyde <u>hates</u> that he <u>needs</u> Jekyll and wants to be a separate person.

2) As Hyde becomes <u>stronger</u>, Jekyll begins to <u>hate</u> "the brute that slept" within him. This may reflect Jekyll's <u>self-loathing</u> — he <u>hates</u> the fact that he has an <u>evil side</u>.

3) Hyde "<u>resented</u> the <u>dislike</u>" which Jekyll feels towards him and <u>punishes</u> Jekyll by playing tricks on him. This may be a <u>warning</u> that it's better to lead a <u>balanced</u> life rather than <u>deny</u> your bad side <u>completely</u>.

Jekyll is not an innocent victim...

Jekyll <u>enjoys indulging</u> his evil side without having to deal with the <u>consequences</u>:

- He's clearly <u>delighted</u> at the thought of pleasure <u>without</u> shame — he "<u>smiled</u> at the notion" and finds it "<u>humorous</u>". He makes thorough <u>arrangements</u>, such as furnishing a house for Hyde, so that he can indulge in his evil side.

- Although Jekyll is <u>shocked</u> by the actions of Hyde and feels "<u>remorse</u>", his "<u>conscience slumbered</u>" because he felt it was "<u>Hyde alone</u>" who was <u>guilty</u>.

- Jekyll knows what Hyde is <u>capable</u> of and that he might one day <u>take over Jekyll</u>, but he isn't strong enough to <u>stop</u> it — he <u>enjoys</u> being Hyde too much.

Writer's Techniques — Language

Jekyll's language shows how he <u>enjoys</u> the <u>freedom</u> of being Hyde. He describes himself as like a "<u>schoolboy</u>", throwing off society's constraints and jumping in the "sea of <u>liberty</u>".

Theme — Dual Nature of Man

The fact Hyde eventually takes over makes you wonder if there was <u>more bad than good</u> in Jekyll after all.

...but we still feel sorry for him

1) In the end, Jekyll <u>admits</u> that his experiment <u>failed</u> — he realises that it <u>isn't possible</u> to cast off man's evil side because it "returns upon us with more <u>unfamiliar</u> and more <u>awful pressure</u>." This contrasts with his earlier <u>pride</u> and <u>excitement</u> at the results of his experiment.

2) It's possible to feel <u>sympathy</u> for Jekyll because he's presented as an <u>ordinary</u> man dealing with some <u>challenging issues</u> of <u>human nature</u>.

3) The reader's sympathy for Jekyll is <u>increased</u> by the <u>horror</u> of his fate. He says that he's facing <u>punishment</u> and that "no one has ever <u>suffered</u> such <u>torments</u>".

© Nick Collinge @ Love It Studios

Mention that Jekyll and Hyde aren't complete opposites...

This will show that you really understand Jekyll's character. Jekyll isn't completely good, and elements of Jekyll can be seen in Hyde — which is evidence of Jekyll's failure to distance himself from his dark side.

Character Profile — Gabriel Utterson

If you were to look up "Victorian gentleman" in the dictionary, a picture of this guy would frown back at you.

Utterson is a man of reason...

1) Utterson is a typically <u>rational</u> Victorian gentleman — he's "a lover of the <u>sane</u> and <u>customary</u> sides of life".

2) He's a <u>lawyer</u> and he approaches the mystery in the same way he'd approach a <u>case</u>. He weighs up the <u>evidence</u> and tries to reach a balanced, unbiased evaluation of the facts.

3) He's <u>unwilling</u> to consider any explanation which <u>threatens</u> to <u>upset</u> his rational way of thinking. He concludes that Jekyll has locked himself in the cabinet because he's suffering from a disease — he thinks this is a "<u>plain</u> and <u>natural</u>" explanation, unlike Poole's murder theory.

Mr Utterson is...

Serious: "a rugged countenance, that was never lighted by a smile"

Reputable: "the last good influence in the lives of down-going men"

Brave: "I shall consider it my duty to break in that door"

...but the disturbing nature of the mystery does affect him

Utterson <u>doesn't suspect</u> a <u>supernatural</u> explanation, although he's <u>aware</u> that something <u>strange</u> is going on:

- Enfield's story about Hyde gives Utterson <u>nightmares</u> — Utterson says that Hyde has "engaged or rather <u>enslaved</u>" his <u>imagination</u> instead of affecting him on a purely <u>intellectual</u> level.

- Utterson feels "<u>mental perplexity</u>" when he meets Hyde for the first time — he's <u>confused</u> because it's <u>impossible</u> to use <u>reason</u> to make sense of something that has a <u>supernatural explanation</u>.

- The memory of Hyde makes Utterson feel a "shudder in his blood". The supernatural nature of Hyde is <u>strong</u> enough to affect Utterson's <u>emotions</u>, which he usually tries to <u>control</u>.

He's curious about Hyde

1) There's something about Hyde that <u>particularly</u> <u>affects</u> Utterson. He feels "a singularly <u>strong</u>, almost an <u>inordinate</u>, <u>curiosity</u>" to see Hyde and he does everything he can to do so — he waits outside the door "by all lights and at all hours".

2) Without Utterson's <u>interest</u> in the mystery, the reader would <u>never</u> get to the bottom of things. However, there are <u>several reasons</u> why Utterson is so interested in Hyde:

© Nick Collinge @ Love It Studios

- To Utterson, <u>maintaining reputation</u> is very <u>important</u>, so he's <u>shocked</u> that Jekyll is willing to harm his reputation for Hyde. Utterson wants to find out <u>why</u> Jekyll is doing this so that he can <u>help</u> him.

- Utterson is <u>frustrated</u> by the <u>mystery</u> surrounding Hyde and wants to use <u>reason</u> to <u>solve</u> it. He wants to see Hyde's face, believing that the mystery will <u>roll away</u> if it's "<u>well examined</u>".

- It's possible that Utterson sees something of his own <u>darker side</u> in Hyde and is <u>strangely drawn</u> to him. As the reader is also made to feel <u>curious</u> about the mystery surrounding Hyde, Stevenson may be suggesting that we are all <u>drawn</u> to the <u>darker</u> side of life and can see the <u>temptation</u> of it.

Character Profile — Gabriel Utterson

He represses his desires

© Nick Collinge @ Love It Studios

1) Utterson is described as "austere" — he's <u>strict</u> with himself and doesn't allow himself many <u>pleasures</u>. For example, he <u>enjoys</u> the theatre but hasn't been to one for <u>twenty years</u>.

2) He doesn't <u>smile</u> much and is "<u>cold</u>" and "<u>dreary</u>". He has a more <u>human side</u> but doesn't let it show in his speech.

3) People enjoy his <u>company</u> because his "rich <u>silence</u>" is <u>calming</u> after the "strain" of making light-hearted conversation. He's a <u>model</u> of Victorian <u>restraint</u>.

> **Background and Context**
>
> These <u>negative descriptions</u> could be <u>criticising</u> the way Victorian gentlemen <u>repressed</u> their emotions.

He's obsessed with reputation...

1) Utterson wants to maintain <u>respectability</u>, <u>order</u> and <u>propriety</u> — when Poole asks Utterson for help and takes him back to Jekyll's house, Utterson calls the servants' distress at Jekyll's behaviour "very <u>unseemly</u>".

2) He's aware of the importance of <u>reputation</u>, which is why he's so <u>concerned</u> for Jekyll's good name — after Carew's murder, Utterson's concern is that Jekyll's name might appear at the <u>trial</u>.

> **Theme — Dual Nature of Man**
>
> The truth about Jekyll and Hyde is more shocking than Utterson suspects, because it means that the <u>appearance</u> of respectability <u>hides</u> a much <u>darker truth</u> about the reality of <u>human nature</u>.

3) He doesn't <u>gossip</u> or go against his sense of <u>restraint</u> to discover the <u>truth</u>. He doesn't read Lanyon's letter out of "professional honour". This partly <u>hampers</u> his <u>ability</u> to <u>solve</u> the mystery — he doesn't want to find out something that will <u>harm</u> Jekyll's reputation.

...but he's tolerant of man's darker side

> **Background and Context**
>
> Utterson's <u>human side</u> shows itself in the "acts of his life" — his <u>tolerance</u>. If Victorian society was more tolerant of human behaviour, there would be <u>less need</u> to <u>hide</u> immoral desires.

1) Although reputation is important to Utterson, he <u>isn't judgemental</u>.

2) He's <u>loyal</u> to those who get into trouble and tries to <u>help</u> them — he tells Jekyll that "Carew was my client, but so are you". Even though Utterson <u>plays</u> by <u>society's rules</u>, he's <u>understanding</u> when people <u>fall foul</u> of them.

3) Utterson has a <u>complicated</u> attitude towards his own <u>dark side</u>:

- Although his past was "<u>fairly blameless</u>", he feels <u>bad</u> for what he <u>views</u> as the "many ill things" he's done — like Jekyll, Utterson sets himself <u>high standards</u> by avoiding what he sees as <u>sinful</u> behaviour.

- He's been <u>tempted</u> to sin and feels a strange "<u>envy</u>" for those who can <u>indulge</u> in their misdeeds — but he doesn't want to <u>harm</u> his reputation so he feels <u>grateful</u> to have avoided committing more sins.

KEY QUOTE

"If your master...is dead, we may at least save his credit"

Utterson loves the 3 R's — Reason, Reputation and Respectability. He doesn't stop going on about them for the whole novel. Even at the end, when there's a weird tiny dead man on the floor in massive clothes.

Character Profile — Dr Hastie Lanyon

Lanyon appears only briefly, but his narrative helps solve the mystery. Gold star to him. Utterson, go home.

Dr Lanyon is an upper-class gentleman

1) At first, Dr Lanyon is described as a "hearty, healthy, dapper, red-faced gentleman" who is <u>friendly</u> and <u>sociable</u>. When Utterson goes to see him he "sprang up from his chair and welcomed him with both hands."

2) This makes him seem <u>larger than life</u>. His friendliness seems "<u>theatrical</u>", which might suggest that he's putting on a front, but it has "<u>genuine feeling</u>" behind it.

> **Dr Lanyon is...**
>
> **Faithful**: "I felt bound to do as he requested"
>
> **Friendly**: "welcomed him with both hands"
>
> **Conventional**: "Jekyll became too fanciful for me"

He's a rational scientist

1) Lanyon has quite a lot <u>in common</u> with Jekyll — they're both doctors and are both <u>respected</u> men. They were also "<u>inseparable</u> friends."

2) However, they have <u>very different</u> views on <u>science</u>. Lanyon deals with <u>rational</u> science in the material world while Jekyll experiments with science of a <u>mystical</u> or <u>supernatural</u> nature.

3) Lanyon regards this as "<u>unscientific balderdash</u>", and Jekyll thinks Lanyon is an "<u>ignorant</u> blatant pedant" for being so <u>sceptical</u>. As a result, the two men aren't as <u>close</u> as they used to be.

© Nick Collinge @ Love It Studios

Lanyon can't cope with Jekyll's supernatural secret

1) Like <u>Utterson</u>, Lanyon <u>never comes close</u> to guessing the truth about Jekyll and Hyde. He finds Jekyll's letter asking Lanyon to retrieve his drugs <u>strange</u> — as a man of <u>reason</u> he concludes that Jekyll is suffering from a "cerebral disease".

2) In the same way that <u>Jekyll</u> was <u>tempted</u> by scientific knowledge, Lanyon allows himself to <u>watch</u> Hyde take the potion, saying that he's "gone too far" not to find out the truth. This shows that he's also tempted by <u>knowledge</u>.

> **Writer's Techniques — Dialogue**
>
> Lanyon's <u>shock</u> is shown by the <u>breakdown</u> of his <u>language</u> — he repeatedly screams "O God!" as he watches Hyde transform into Jekyll.

3) Jekyll shows Lanyon <u>evidence</u> of the supernatural that he can't ignore. Lanyon <u>can't cope</u> with the truth of what Jekyll has done — his whole <u>world view</u> is turned <u>upside down</u> by Jekyll's discovery. His "<u>soul sickened</u>", which shows the depth of his shock. He <u>dies</u> because he can't recover from such a <u>revelation</u>.

EXAM TIP

Compare and contrast different characters...

It will impress the examiner if you can analyse the characters in relation to each other. Jekyll and Lanyon are both respectable gentlemen, but they represent two opposing attitudes when it comes to science.

Character Profile — Mr Enfield & Poole

On to minor characters now and yet another Victorian gentleman. And a doting butler, for a bit of variety.

Enfield has the same Victorian values as Utterson...

1) Enfield is a distant cousin of Utterson. Although he's only a <u>minor</u> character, he plays an <u>important</u> part in the novel — he <u>introduces</u> Utterson to the <u>mystery</u> around Hyde through his initial story.

2) He embodies typical <u>Victorian values</u>:

> • He understands the <u>importance</u> of <u>reputation</u>. He <u>pressures</u> Hyde into paying for his crime by <u>threatening</u> to "make his name <u>stink</u> from one end of London to the other."
>
> • He says he doesn't like to <u>gossip</u> because gossip can <u>negatively</u> affect a person's reputation. He's "<u>ashamed</u>" of his "<u>long tongue</u>" after he tells Utterson about Hyde.

...but the two characters are very different

1) Enfield and Utterson don't have much in <u>common</u>. People wonder "what these two could see in each other", but to them their meetings are the "<u>chief jewel</u>" of each week". This doesn't necessarily say anything <u>positive</u> about Enfield's character — we're told that Utterson is <u>loyal</u> to those he's known the <u>longest</u>, like Enfield.

> **Theme — Dual Nature of Man**
>
> Utterson and Enfield are <u>drawn together</u> despite their apparent <u>differences</u>. This links to Jekyll and Hyde and the idea that <u>differences</u> can be <u>brought together</u>.

2) There's a hint that Enfield has an <u>immoral side</u>. He's returning "from <u>some place</u> at the end of the world" at <u>3 am</u> when he sees Hyde trample the child — we're left to <u>speculate</u> where he's been.

3) Unlike Utterson, Enfield <u>isn't curious</u> at all about Hyde. He makes sure that Hyde pays for his crime, but he <u>isn't interested</u> in asking any <u>questions</u> about Jekyll and the cheque — he says "the more it looks like Queer Street, <u>the less I ask</u>". This could be a comment on Victorian society — everyone <u>knew</u> that everyone else was <u>secretly sinning</u>, so didn't ask too many <u>questions</u>.

Poole is loyal to Jekyll

1) Poole has been Jekyll's butler for <u>twenty years</u> — he knows his master's habits well and <u>recognises</u> when something is <u>badly wrong</u>. This makes <u>Utterson's reluctance</u> to believe him straight away look <u>unreasonable</u>.

2) Poole sees Jekyll as a <u>respectable</u> man, so he'd rather believe that he's been murdered than consider any other, darker explanation.

3) Poole <u>cares</u> about Jekyll. He's <u>concerned</u> by his strange behaviour — he's very <u>anxious</u> when he goes to ask Utterson for help and he <u>bravely</u> helps to knock the cabinet door down. This reflects <u>well</u> on Jekyll's character because it shows that he's <u>worthy</u> of concern.

© Nick Collinge @ Love It Studios

EXAM TIP

Don't forget to write about minor characters...

Don't just write about the main characters — minor characters are important because they move the plot along and contribute to the themes of the novel. Writing about them will show that you know your stuff.

Practice Questions

There aren't loads of characters in 'Jekyll and Hyde', but the ones who <u>are</u> in it are pretty complex — with Jekyll, you get two characters for the price of one, you lucky things. It's important to know what these characters are like, their role in the novel and why they do the crazy things they do. These lovely questions will help...

Quick Questions

1) Give one example to show that Jekyll fits in with respectable society.

2) Why does Jekyll think that his sins are worse than they are?

3) Which three words best describe Hyde?
   a) Respectable   b) Evil   c) Animalistic   d) Distinguished   e) Cruel

4) Write down two of Hyde's physical features that people find disturbing.

5) Find a quote from the text that shows that Utterson is a rational man.

6) Give one reason why Utterson is so interested in Hyde.

7) Give one similarity and one difference between Lanyon and Jekyll.

8) Why is Lanyon, as a scientist, so shocked by Jekyll's discovery?

9) Give two examples that show how Enfield's character reflects Victorian values.

10) What is Poole's job?

Practice Questions

If you're an ambitious character like Jekyll, you might be pondering the possibility of separating off your slothful side so your hardworking side can answer these questions. Don't. You've seen what can happen and it was messy. If you get on with practising writing longer answers now, it'll be a doddle come exam time.

In-depth Questions

1) Describe Jekyll's character.
   Use quotes to back up your answer.

2) Find three examples where Stevenson describes Hyde as being like an animal in the novel.

3) Describe Jekyll's attitude to science in the novel.

4) Give two ways that Hyde is the opposite of Jekyll. Use quotes from the novel in your answer.

5) Compare Jekyll's attitude to Hyde:
   a) when he turns into Hyde for the first time   b) after Carew's murder.

6) In what ways does Utterson repress his desires?

7) Explain Utterson's attitude to his darker side and the darker side of others.

8) Compare Lanyon's character when we first meet him to his character after he learns Jekyll's secret.

9) How does Stevenson use Enfield to explore the theme of the dual nature of man?

10) List three reasons why Poole is concerned about Jekyll.

Practice Questions

It's time for the third course — tasty Exam-style questions. It's a good idea to do them in exam conditions as it'll make a silent exam hall seem much less daunting. If you really want to improve your essay writing skills, come back to the answers you've written to these questions later on and try to improve them.

Exam-style Questions

1) Using the passage below as a starting point, explore how Utterson's character influences the way he approaches the mystery.

> Taken from 'The Last Night'
>
> "These are all very strange circumstances," said Mr Utterson, "but I think I begin to see daylight. Your master, Poole, is plainly seized with one of those maladies that both torture and deform the sufferer; hence, for aught I know, the alteration of his voice; hence the mask and his avoidance of his friends; hence his eagerness to find this drug, by means of which the poor soul retains some hope of ultimate recovery - God grant that he be not deceived! There is my explanation; it is sad enough, Poole, ay, and appalling to consider; but it is plain and natural, hangs well together and delivers us from all exorbitant alarms."
>
> "Sir," said the butler, turning to a sort of mottled pallor, "that thing was not my master, and there's the truth. My master" — here he looked round him and began to whisper — "is a tall fine man, and this was more of a dwarf." Utterson attempted to protest. "O, sir," cried Poole, do you think I do not know my master after twenty years? do you think I do not know where his head comes to in the cabinet door, where I saw him every morning of my life? No, sir, that thing in the mask was never Doctor Jekyll — God knows what it was, but it was never Doctor Jekyll; and it is the belief of my heart that there was murder done."
>
> "Poole," replied the lawyer, "if you say that, it will become my duty to make certain. Much as I desire to spare your master's feelings, much as I am puzzled by this note which seems to prove him to be still alive, I shall consider it my duty to break in that door."

2) How does Stevenson use descriptions and imagery to present Hyde as an evil character?

3) To what extent does Stevenson present Jekyll as a sympathetic character?

4) Describe how the relationship between Jekyll and Hyde changes throughout the novel.

Section Three — Characters

Reputation

Before you tackle this page, you might want to cast your mind back to page 6. It's a good'un, trust me.

Victorian society expected gentlemen to have a good reputation

1) Reputation is very <u>important</u> to the gentlemen in the novel:

> <u>Immoral activities</u> and <u>uncontrolled emotions</u> would <u>damage</u> a gentleman's <u>reputation</u>. If this happened, they may no longer be seen as a gentleman at all, which would mean <u>losing</u> many <u>social advantages</u> (see p.6). This means that the gentlemen in *Jekyll and Hyde* <u>value</u> their reputations <u>above all else</u>.

2) Utterson is <u>wary</u> of <u>gossip</u>, in case it <u>reflects badly</u> on him or his friends. He and Enfield agree <u>never</u> to <u>talk</u> about Hyde, and believe in <u>not asking questions</u> if something "looks like Queer Street".

3) Utterson is more <u>concerned</u> about <u>preserving</u> Jekyll's <u>reputation</u> than bringing Hyde to trial. After Carew's murder, he says to Jekyll, "If it came to a trial, <u>your name</u> might appear."

© Nick Collinge @ Love It Studios

4) Stevenson's message is that <u>reputations</u> cannot be <u>trusted</u> because they are based on <u>appearances</u>. They are the version of a person that he or she <u>wants</u> the <u>world</u> to <u>see</u>.

5) When a <u>society</u> values <u>reputation</u> as highly as the Victorians did, it makes it difficult to know what people are <u>really</u> like. This is what causes <u>Utterson</u> problems — he <u>cannot</u> fully <u>understand</u> Jekyll's situation because he <u>only</u> sees Jekyll's <u>reputation</u> as <u>important</u>. This means that he holds onto the idea of <u>blackmail</u> until the very last moment — he finds it <u>hard</u> to look <u>beyond</u> his concern for reputation.

Jekyll is more worried about his reputation than his sins

1) Jekyll has to hide his sins to protect his reputation. He <u>struggles</u> with this, so he creates Hyde to rid himself of the "<u>disgrace</u>" of sin. Jekyll's feelings are shown by the following quote:

This simile makes Jekyll seem quite childish and irresponsible.

Jekyll still wants a gentlemanly reputation.

He associates Hyde with freedom.

> I was the first that could thus plod in the public eye with a load of genial respectability, and in a moment, like a schoolboy, strip off these lendings and spring headlong into the sea of liberty. But for me, in my impenetrable mantle, the safety was complete. Think of it — I did not even exist!

Jekyll thinks his reputation is safe.

He sees Hyde as a different person because it makes him feel better.

2) This quote shows how concerned Jekyll is with his <u>reputation</u> — he thinks more about <u>hiding</u> his sins than <u>dealing</u> with them. He feels <u>free</u> as Hyde because he can conceal his sins <u>perfectly</u>.

"I had been safe of all men's respect"

Jekyll gets a little carried away with his 'goodie by day, baddie by night' arrangement. He can prowl around in the dark causing death and destruction, whilst his reputation remains intact. Ideal. Until it goes wrong.

Dual Nature of Man

This is probably the most important theme in the novel, so make sure you've got plenty to say about it.

Jekyll believes there are two sides to every individual

1) <u>Before</u> he creates Hyde, Jekyll feels that he is leading a <u>double life</u>:

- Jekyll is an <u>established gentleman</u>, with "the <u>respect</u> of the <u>wise</u> and <u>good</u>" in society.

- On the other hand, he is guilty of "<u>irregularities</u>" — sins and desires that he keeps <u>hidden</u>.

2) Jekyll decides that this <u>duality</u> applies to <u>all of humanity</u>: "man is not truly one, but <u>truly two</u>." Jekyll states this as fact, because he's so <u>convinced</u> he's right. This leads him to risk everything.

3) Jekyll is more <u>self-aware</u> than the other characters. He feels like the good and evil sides of his personality are <u>struggling</u> against one another, and decides to <u>take action</u> by separating them. However, he <u>fails</u> to fully separate his two sides because he is "radically both".

> **Writer's Techniques — Language**
>
> Stevenson uses the <u>language of battle</u> to describe the struggle. There's a "<u>war</u>" within Jekyll, and the "two natures that <u>contended in the field</u>" of his mind sound like two forces meeting on a battlefield.

4) Jekyll <u>underestimates</u> how closely the good and bad sides of his personality are <u>bound</u> <u>together</u>. He also underestimates the <u>power</u> and <u>attraction</u> of his purely evil side — in the end, Hyde and the bad part of Jekyll <u>outweigh</u> the good part of Jekyll.

The two sides can be seen as sinful and virtuous

1) Without Hyde, Jekyll lives a <u>virtuous</u> life and is "<u>distinguished for religion</u>" and charity. But he is also an "<u>ordinary secret sinner</u>". All people, including Jekyll, are a <u>mixture</u> of sin and virtue.

2) In contrast, Hyde is the purely satanic side of Jekyll. He writes all over Jekyll's religious text with "<u>startling blasphemies</u>". Jekyll calls Hyde "<u>My devil</u>", and Utterson thinks that "<u>Satan's signature</u>" is written on Hyde's face.

> Hyde is created because of Jekyll's desire to <u>rid</u> himself of sin, rather than <u>deal with</u> it. Jekyll says that Hyde could have been created as "<u>an angel instead of a fiend</u>", if only the experiment had been done with more "<u>pious</u>" intentions (i.e. for God's glory, not his own).

3) Although Stevenson shows the dangers of letting this <u>sinful</u> side take over, the novel also shows <u>complex attitudes</u> to sin:

- it's <u>tempting</u> — Jekyll feels "<u>younger, lighter, happier</u>" as Hyde.

- it's <u>powerful</u> — Hyde <u>takes over</u> in the end.

- it's <u>unavoidable</u> — as Hyde, Jekyll gives in to "<u>original evil</u>".

> **Background and Context — Religion**
>
> In this period, a branch of Christianity called <u>Evangelicalism</u> taught that all mankind are <u>inevitably sinful</u>, because Adam and Eve sinned. Stevenson <u>frightens</u> his readers by taking this <u>further</u> — the sinful side isn't only inevitable, it can also be <u>stronger</u>.

For more on religion in Victorian times, see p.8.

© Nick Collinge @ Love It Studios

Dual Nature of Man

The two sides can be seen as civilised and uncivilised

1) Hyde isn't just the sinful side of Jekyll — he's also the <u>uncivilised</u> side. He <u>disrupts</u> the ordered, civilised world that Jekyll and his friends live in.

2) Some upper-class Victorians thought that people who committed <u>crimes</u>, or disrupted the social order, were <u>less evolved</u>. They tried to use <u>Darwin's</u> theory of evolution to back this up.

3) Stevenson forces his readers to consider the possibility that there's a <u>savage</u> within all people, even if they seemed <u>civilised</u>. Hyde behaves "<u>like a madman</u>" and is "<u>ape-like</u>", but he's a part of Jekyll. This suggests that it is the <u>civilised</u> side of Jekyll's personality that exercises <u>restraint</u> — without it, all that is left is the pure <u>evil</u> of Hyde.

There's more about Darwin on page 8.

Background and Context

Darwin argued that humans shared a common <u>ancestor</u> with <u>apes</u>. Some upper-class Victorians accepted his theory of evolution, but interpreted it in a <u>different way</u> — they felt evolution would eventually lead to the creation of a '<u>perfect</u>' creature (and on this basis, they saw themselves as <u>more highly evolved</u> than the rest of society).

Character — Poole

This also applies to <u>other</u> characters to a certain extent. Poole is a <u>loyal</u>, "<u>well-dressed</u>" servant, but he <u>shouts</u> at another servant with "<u>ferocity</u>".

Stevenson uses man's dual nature to comment on society

1) Stevenson uses the idea of duality to <u>criticise respectable society</u>. He suggests that the <u>gap</u> between <u>appearance</u> and <u>reality</u> in the people and places of Victorian London is <u>hypocritical</u>.

Hypocrisy is the act of pretending to have standards or beliefs, but not actually living by them.

2) Jekyll appears respectable, until he puts on the "<u>thick cloak</u>" of Hyde. This is mirrored in Jekyll's <u>house</u> — it "<u>wore</u> a great air of wealth and comfort" from the front, but it is secretly <u>connected</u> to the <u>shabby</u> door to the laboratory. Stevenson uses <u>imagery</u> of <u>clothing</u> to show how <u>people</u> and <u>places</u> can put forward a <u>misleading appearance</u> to the world.

3) Characters are proud of their <u>reputations</u>, so they prioritise the <u>appearance</u> of respectability over <u>honesty</u>. The <u>gentlemanly</u> characters look down on <u>immoral</u> activities in <u>public</u>, and then do them anyway (most obviously in Jekyll's case). <u>Stevenson</u> shows that this behaviour can have terrible <u>consequences</u> — <u>Jekyll's fate</u> is a <u>warning</u> about trying to <u>hide</u> who you are.

Background and Context — Victorian Gentlemen

Victorian society had a <u>particularly rigid</u> set of moral values. To maintain a good reputation, gentlemen had to repress <u>many</u> of their <u>true feelings and desires</u> in public (see p.33).

© Nick Collinge @ Love It Studios

4) In contrast, Hyde's <u>evil</u> nature is <u>shown clearly</u> in his "displeasing smile" and "extraordinary appearance". He is the only one who doesn't <u>hide</u> behind <u>appearances</u> — <u>Stevenson</u> may be suggesting that appearances can only conceal <u>so much</u>.

"I learned...the thorough and primitive duality of man"

Jekyll struggles to reconcile the good and evil sides of himself, so he creates Hyde to get rid of the evil bit. Hyde's kind of like that little voice in your head that says, "Eat the biscuits. Eat them. Eat them all."

Science and Religion

There are some tricky ideas about science and religion in the novel, but don't let that put you off. Use Section One to get your head around the context, and then have a gander at these lovely pages of facts and fun.

The characters are interested in science and religion

For more on science and religion in the Victorian period, see page 8.

1) Jekyll and Lanyon are scientists. Their profession relies on rational methods and hard evidence.

2) They live in a Christian society. Jekyll is fond of religious texts, and often calls on God to help him.

3) Lanyon and Jekyll have very different approaches to science and religion:

Lanyon keeps science and religion separate	Jekyll combines science and religion
• Lanyon deals with the science of the material world. • He cannot cope with Jekyll using scientific research to experiment with spiritual matters.	• Jekyll's scientific work leads "wholly towards the mystic and the transcendental". • He uses science to deal with "that hard law of life, which lies at the root of religion". The "hard law" is the idea that all humans are sinful.

4) The tension between science and religion was a source of conflict in Victorian society:

- At the start of the nineteenth century most people believed the explanation from the Bible that the earth was created by God. However, throughout the nineteenth century, scientists began to disprove this theory — they believed that the world was created by a process of evolution.

- Many Victorians thought this view was dangerous because it suggested that science had the power to create life. It challenged their religious view of the world.

Religion is a social issue as well as a personal one

1) Christianity teaches that everyone is sinful. Hyde was created because Jekyll was so troubled by his sins, even though they weren't actually that bad. When he was younger, he "regarded and hid them with an almost morbid sense of shame."

2) Being seen to do good or charitable deeds, on the other hand, is another sign of respectability. After Hyde murders Carew, Jekyll becomes "distinguished for religion" for a few months — he's known for doing good deeds.

3) Stevenson criticises the act of being religious in public and sinful in private, by presenting Jekyll's actions as hypocritical.

Character — Jekyll

Jekyll finds it easy to put on a show of doing good deeds, but doesn't deal with his guilty conscience (because he thinks it's "Hyde alone, that was guilty"). This allows Hyde to gain in strength, and in the end Jekyll is destroyed.

Writer's Techniques — Language

Stevenson reminds the reader that Jekyll's actions are sinful by using religious language. For example, Jekyll is a "secret sinner" and Hyde is "the spirit of hell".

© Nick Collinge @ Love It Studios

Science and Religion

Science is sometimes portrayed as unsettling

Stevenson presents Jekyll's scientific work as mysterious and disturbing:

- The transformation of Hyde to Jekyll is hideous. Lanyon finds it sickening, and Jekyll describes his first transformation as provoking "racking pangs", "deadly nausea" and "a horror of the spirit".

- Jekyll's cabinet is full of curious objects that Utterson and Poole don't understand. There are "traces" of chemicals, "various" measures of "some white salt", and they decide the cheval glass has seen "some strange things". Stevenson uses this vague language to present science as mysterious.

Science is shown to be powerful

1) Jekyll's science causes death and destruction. This shows how powerful science can be when it's used to upset the conventional order of Victorian life.

2) Jekyll says that the details of his experiment cannot be shared for two reasons:

- Jekyll says he won't "deeply" describe his experiment because it caused his evil side to return with a "more awful pressure." This acts as a warning about the power of science.

- His experiment was also "incomplete." Even Jekyll, a respected scientist, failed to achieve his aims, and he couldn't control the power of the evil he unleashed.

Writer's Techniques — Language

Jekyll's drugs "shook the doors of the prisonhouse of [his] disposition". This strong language shows that Jekyll feels the sinful side of his personality was trapped by the more respectable side.

Jekyll's science goes against religious beliefs

Christianity was an important part of Victorian society.

1) It is the "temptation of a discovery so singular and profound" that motivates Jekyll to create Hyde. He tries to change human nature, which Christians see as God's creation.

2) Jekyll meddles with human nature for his own selfish reasons. He doesn't have good intentions — this means that Jekyll creates an evil, rather than good, alter ego.

3) Despite this, Jekyll has still made a scientific breakthrough. He repeats the phrase "I was the first...", showing how proud he is of himself. He starts to think he is "beyond the reach of fate."

Background and Context — Religion

The language of torment that Jekyll uses links to the Christian idea of Hell — a place in the afterlife of constant suffering.

4) But this is not the case. By the end, Jekyll is the "chief of sufferers", and experiences "torments" as Hyde grows in strength.

Show that you understand that Jekyll's experiment failed...

Instead of one good and one evil side, Jekyll just creates an evil side, and he stays a mix of both. Don't write 'Jekyll = good, Hyde = evil'. Science is a powerful thing that even Jekyll can't master.

Secrecy

The gentlemen in *Jekyll and Hyde* are a pretty secretive bunch, even though they're supposed to be friends.

There are a lot of secrets in the novel

The <u>whole plot</u> of *Jekyll and Hyde* revolves around Jekyll's <u>secret alter ego</u>, but <u>other characters</u> also have secrets:

> **Writer's Techniques — Narrative**
>
> Stevenson's narrative has many <u>gaps</u> — this makes the reader more suspicious of things that are left <u>unspoken</u> or <u>unexplained</u>.

- <u>Utterson</u> has done "<u>many ill things</u>" in his past, but he doesn't say what these are. This makes his actions appear <u>shameful</u>, even though his past is "<u>fairly blameless</u>".

- It's never explained where <u>Enfield</u> was returning from at three o'clock in the morning. This makes the reader more likely to <u>assume</u> that he was somewhere <u>scandalous</u>.

Many things are left unsaid

© United Archives GmbH / Alamy

1) The gentlemen characters often decide <u>not to speak</u> about unpleasant things so they can <u>pretend</u> they're not happening (for example, Utterson and Enfield agree never to talk about Hyde again).

> **Character — Jekyll**
>
> Jekyll <u>can't speak</u> about Hyde, perhaps because he <u>can't admit</u> to his <u>origin</u> as part of Jekyll. He asks Utterson to "respect" his silence, and says he "<u>cannot share</u>" what he knows.

2) They also <u>downplay</u> shocking events. For example, Enfield describes the trampled girl as "<u>a bad story</u>", and when Lanyon says he regards Jekyll as dead, Utterson's only reply is "<u>Tut-tut</u>". This <u>understatement</u> shows that the gentlemen are determined to pretend that everything is <u>normal</u>.

3) Both Lanyon and Jekyll choose to <u>write</u> about their experiences, rather than speak about them. These letters are left <u>unread</u> until the end of the novel, which adds to the <u>secrecy</u> and <u>suspense</u>.

Stevenson uses locked doors as symbols

See pages 44 and 45 for more on setting.

1) There are many <u>closed doors</u> and <u>windows</u> in the novel:

- The <u>back door</u> to Jekyll's house has "<u>neither bell nor knocker</u>" and it's associated with <u>Hyde</u>.

- Jekyll <u>slams</u> the window <u>shut</u> on Utterson and Enfield, and later <u>locks</u> himself in the cabinet.

- Important items, like <u>letters</u> and Jekyll's <u>ingredients</u>, are kept securely <u>locked</u> in drawers and safes.

2) These closed doors and windows <u>represent</u> people's <u>desire to hide</u> their secrets, so <u>smashing</u> the cabinet door is a <u>symbolic moment</u>. It represents the <u>breakdown</u> of Jekyll's walls of <u>secrecy</u>.

Write about different ways that Stevenson creates secrecy...

Show the examiner that you understand Stevenson's different techniques — he creates secrecy using gaps in the <u>narrative</u>, the gentlemen's <u>language</u>, and the <u>settings</u>. Have a look at Section Five for more on all this.

Practice Questions

Phew, that was a pretty chunky section. Now you've got an idea of how the main themes work in 'Jekyll and Hyde', it's a good idea to go back to the novel and find examples for yourself. Maybe go wild and jot down a few notes about them. Then have a go at these Quick Questions to check that you've taken it all in.

Quick Questions

1) What is Utterson worrying about when he says to Jekyll, "If it came to a trial, your name might appear"?

2) Is the following statement true or false?
   Jekyll first starts to feel like he is leading a double life after he has created Hyde.

3) Find a quote from the novel that suggests that Hyde is:
   a) the sinful side of Jekyll.
   b) the uncivilised side of Jekyll.

4) What is Lanyon's attitude towards Jekyll's scientific work?

5) Give an example from the novel of how science is portrayed as:
   a) unsettling.
   b) powerful.

6) Give one example of how Jekyll's experiment goes against Christianity.

7) In what way is Jekyll's experiment a failure?

8) Give an example of the secretive behaviour of each of these characters:
   a) Mr Enfield
   b) Mr Utterson

9) Why do Utterson and Enfield agree not to speak about Hyde?

10) Give one example of when a gentleman plays down something uncivilised in the novel.

Practice Questions

These In-depth Questions take a little more thinking about, but it's well worth the time and effort. It's much better to ask yourself these questions now than in the exam, when you'll be more pushed for time. Try to write about a paragraph for each one, and include some quotes from the text to support your answers.

In-depth Questions

1) How does Stevenson suggest that reputations cannot be trusted? Give some examples from the text.

2) Which character in the novel do you think is most concerned about reputation? Explain your answer.

3) To what extent is Jekyll's experiment successful? Give some examples from the novel to back up your answer.

4) Henry Jekyll is the most obviously divided character in the novel. Pick one other character in *Jekyll and Hyde*, and explain how Stevenson shows that they have two sides to their personality.

5) Explain the differences between Lanyon's and Jekyll's attitudes to science.

6) Briefly explain why religion and science were in conflict in Victorian times.

7) How does Stevenson present the gentlemen in the novel's attitudes to secrecy?

8) Why do you think Utterson leaves Lanyon's letter unread until the end of the novel? Explain your answer.

Practice Questions

Themes are a favourite with examiners, so it's wise to practise writing some essays about them. Try doing these questions under exam conditions, so you get a sense of how much time you'll have for the real thing. You never know — one of these beauties may be really similar to the question you get on the day. How neat that would be.

Exam-style Questions

1) Using the extract below as a starting point, explain how Stevenson presents science in the novel.

> Taken from 'Henry Jekyll's Full Statement of the Case'
>
> I hesitated long before I put this theory to the test of practice. I knew well that I risked death; for any drug that so potently controlled and shook the very fortress of identity, might by the least scruple of an overdose or at the least inopportunity in the moment of exhibition, utterly blot out that immaterial tabernacle which I looked to it to change. But the temptation of a discovery so singular and profound, at last overcame the suggestions of alarm. I had long since prepared my tincture[1]; I purchased at once, from a firm of wholesale chemists, a large quantity of a particular salt which I knew, from my experiments, to be the last ingredient required; and late one accursed night, I compounded the elements, watched them boil and smoke together in the glass, and when the ebullition[2] had subsided, with a strong glow of courage, drank off the potion.
>
> The most racking pangs succeeded: a grinding in the bones, deadly nausea, and a horror of the spirit that cannot be exceeded at the hour of birth or death. Then these agonies began swiftly to subside, and I came to myself as if out of a great sickness. There was something strange in my sensations, something indescribably new and, from its very novelty, incredibly sweet. I felt younger, lighter, happier in body; within I was conscious of a heady recklessness, a current of disordered sensual images running like a mill race in my fancy, a solution of the bonds of obligation, an unknown but not an innocent freedom of the soul. I knew myself, at the first breath of this new life, to be more wicked, tenfold more wicked, sold a slave to my original evil; and the thought, in that moment, braced and delighted me like wine.
>
> [1] tincture — a solution made by dissolving a drug in alcohol
> [2] ebullition — the act of boiling something

2) "Utterson's concern for Jekyll's reputation does them both more harm than good."
   How far would you agree with this view?

3) In his final statement, Jekyll writes that "man is not truly one, but truly two."
   In what ways does Stevenson suggest that Jekyll is right?

4) How does Stevenson use the theme of secrecy to create suspense in the novel?

Structure and Narrative

It's really important to write about structure, because Stevenson uses it to build tension.
Get a few technical terms from these pages under your belt — like 'embedded narrative'. Fancy.

The structure of the narrative builds suspense

1) Most of the story is a <u>third-person</u> narrative, which follows <u>Utterson</u>.
   The narrative is <u>limited</u> — Utterson finds
   things out gradually and only learns the truth
   at the very end. This distances the reader
   from the truth, creating <u>tension</u> and <u>intrigue</u>.

   First-person narrative uses 'I'. Third-person narrative uses 'he', 'she' and 'they'.

© Nick Collinge @ Love It Studios

Character — Utterson

Utterson has an "approved tolerance for others", which suggests that
he won't be judgemental about other characters. This encourages
the reader to rely on his <u>interpretations</u>, because he has a rational,
unbiased attitude. However, there are many things he <u>doesn't know</u>.

2) The main narrative follows Utterson's experiences in <u>chronological</u> order.
   This gives a sense of <u>time passing</u>, increasing <u>tension</u> as time goes on.

3) The last two chapters do <u>not</u> follow a linear structure. Instead, they return
   to explain previous events. By leaving these key <u>explanations</u> until the
   very <u>end</u> of the novel, Stevenson keeps the reader in <u>suspense</u> throughout.

Embedded narratives make the story more authentic

1) Stevenson uses several <u>embedded narratives</u> in the novel. These
   include <u>written documents</u> (like Lanyon's letter and Jekyll's
   statement), and <u>testimonies</u> from characters like Mr Enfield.

   An embedded narrative is a story within the main narrative.

- <u>Enfield's story</u> about the <u>door</u> is important because it's the <u>first hint</u> of a mystery. Enfield says
  it's "<u>a very odd story</u>" before he tells it, which <u>grips</u> the reader's interest from the start.

- The Carew murder is explained through a <u>maid's account</u>. She is "romantically given" and faints
  after witnessing the murder, which shows she is <u>emotional</u>. This makes her account <u>quite limited</u>
  — we feel <u>removed</u> from the events and don't know how much we can <u>trust</u> her narrative.

- Lanyon's <u>first-person</u> narrative is mostly written in <u>formal</u>, <u>measured language</u>, which makes it seem
  more <u>credible</u>. This is important, because it's the <u>first account</u> the reader gets of Jekyll <u>transforming</u>.
  This narrative also has <u>limitations</u>, because Lanyon refuses to write down some of what he's heard.

2) These narratives are <u>pieces of evidence</u> in the case. By including
   them, Stevenson makes the story more <u>realistic</u> (even if parts of it
   seem <u>impossible</u>), which in turn makes it more <u>frightening</u>.

Character — Hyde

The reader never gets a first
person account from Hyde.
He is <u>excluded</u> from the
narrative, as he is from
society. This makes him
seem more <u>mysterious</u>.

The novel's full title is 'The <u>Strange Case</u> of Dr Jekyll and Mr Hyde' and
the <u>chapter titles</u> refer to incidents and statements. This gives the sense of
a real investigation, which <u>contrasts</u> with the fantastical nature of Hyde.

3) The embedded narratives are also a <u>device</u> to add to the reader's <u>curiosity</u>.
   Like a <u>jigsaw</u>, all of the pieces are needed to work out Jekyll's secret.

Structure and Narrative

Documents provide information but also add intrigue

1) Written documents <u>reveal information</u> to certain characters, but Stevenson <u>carefully controls how much</u>.

Jekyll's will

This is a <u>starting point</u> in Utterson's hunt for Mr Hyde. As a legal document, it's authentic <u>evidence</u> of Jekyll's link to Hyde. However, it also <u>poses questions</u> — Enfield's story has already suggested that Hyde is a <u>shady</u> character, so it seems <u>strange</u> that Jekyll, a respected gentleman, would leave him everything.

Carew's letter to Utterson

This is the letter found on Carew's body. The reader never finds out what was written in it. Stevenson leaves these <u>gaps</u> in the narrative to add to the <u>reader's suspicions</u>.

Hyde's letter to Jekyll

This is the letter Jekyll gives Utterson after Carew's murder. Utterson is <u>initially reassured</u> by it, because it implies that Hyde isn't blackmailing Jekyll, but he has his "<u>fears renewed</u>" when Poole insists that it wasn't delivered. This adds <u>intrigue</u>. When Guest examines the handwriting, Utterson assumes that Jekyll is forging for Hyde. This letter is <u>misleading</u>, because Hyde and Jekyll are the same person.

2) Written documents make the story seem <u>more realistic</u>, because different people reveal different parts of the story. They also add <u>suspense</u>, because the information is revealed <u>gradually</u>. The narrative is made more <u>fragmented</u> by these written documents — they offer small <u>hints</u> but not the <u>whole story</u>.

3) Stevenson also suggests that the reader should question the <u>reliability</u> of written documents, by hinting at their authors' <u>secretive behaviour</u>.

Jekyll's final confession fills in the gaps in the story

1) Jekyll's statement <u>recaps</u> everything that's <u>already happened</u> in the novel.

2) It does this in <u>chronological order</u>, going back before Utterson's narrative began, and continuing until shortly before Hyde's death. It's the <u>first time</u> that the previous events have been fully explained.

3) Stevenson uses a <u>first-person</u> narrative for Jekyll's statement, because Jekyll is the <u>only character</u> who knows the <u>whole truth</u>. This gives the reader <u>direct access</u> to his thoughts and feelings.

4) The word '<u>statement</u>' suggests an <u>unbiased</u> report. But it could be difficult for the reader to completely <u>trust</u> what Jekyll writes, because he's already shown that he's capable of <u>deceiving</u> people — even his closest friends. He also leaves some things <u>unexplained</u>, such as the contents of his potion.

"'This is a strange note,' said Mr Utterson."

Many modern readers already know Jekyll's secret, but that wasn't the case for the Victorians, who would've been on tenterhooks until the very end (thanks to Utterson's striking ability to jump to wrong conclusions).

Setting and Symbolism

The settings in *Jekyll and Hyde* are often used for symbolic effect — it's all about reading between the lines.

The novel's settings are mostly dark and foggy

1) Stevenson emphasises the darkness (or partial darkness) in the novel. The less respectable parts of London are especially associated with darkness.

2) For example, in Soho, the light is always changing. Utterson sees "degrees and hues of twilight", a "haggard shaft of daylight" and "changing glimpses" of streets.

3) This symbolises the narrative as a whole — only parts of the truth can be seen at any one time.

4) Stevenson also repeatedly mentions the fog. It's so dense that it covers whole streets, making them places of secrecy.

5) The fog actively works against the characters at times. When Utterson visits Soho, it "cut him off" from his surroundings. Stevenson uses the fog to isolate characters and restrict their view of events.

6) Fog also symbolises mystery. For example, the lecture theatre at Jekyll's house is described as "foggy". The fact that the fog seems to have come indoors represents how deeply Jekyll has hidden his secret.

> Stevenson uses the moon to highlight parts of settings. Carew's murder is "brilliantly lit by the full moon", which makes it more dramatic, as if it's under a spotlight. The moon is also used to add to the spooky atmosphere — in 'The Last Night', the moon is described as "lying on her back". The personification makes it seem as if the whole world has been turned upside down by Jekyll's secret.

> **Background and Context — Victorian London**
>
> Victorian London was known for its smoke. It was so dense that people sometimes fell into the Thames. See p.7.

Stevenson presents London's streets as threatening places

1) The streets of London are presented as dangerous — both of Hyde's attacks take place there.

2) Stevenson carefully builds a nightmarish version of London that's half-way between reality and fiction:

- He uses vague descriptions of familiar settings. For example, Jekyll lives on "some square or other."
- He includes specific details about locations. Jekyll's house is two doors in from the end of the street.
- He mentions place names which didn't exist in London at the time, like Gaunt Street.

3) This makes the setting more frightening for Victorian readers, because it's familiar (see p.48).

4) The streets are often linked to horror and nightmares. Utterson has an actual nightmare in which he imagines a terrifying city of "labyrinths". Soho is described as "a district of some city in a nightmare", as if Utterson's visions have become real.

5) The streets are often empty. When Poole fetches Utterson to Jekyll's house, Utterson feels "he had never seen that part of London so deserted." This is a bustling part of the city, so its emptiness is strange — it's as if the characters are isolated from the busy city in a bubble of silence and mystery. This contributes to Utterson and Poole's anxiety.

> **Character — Hyde**
>
> Hyde is often associated with darkness, which makes him even more mysterious.

Setting and Symbolism

Jekyll's house symbolises his character

1) <u>Like Jekyll himself</u>, Jekyll's house has <u>two sides</u> which are <u>connected</u>:

- The <u>respectable</u> main house is at the <u>front</u> and has an "<u>air of wealth</u>".

- But through a yard at the <u>back</u> there's a laboratory, with a back door that's "<u>blistered and distained</u>."

- This <u>symbolises</u> Jekyll's <u>personality</u> — he's outwardly <u>respectable</u>, but inwardly <u>sinful</u>. The Hyde side of his personality is <u>connected</u> to him, but he keeps it <u>hidden</u> away.

2) After his brief meeting with Utterson, Hyde escapes into the house "<u>with extraordinary quickness</u>" and <u>shuts</u> the door behind him. This suggests that he uses the building to <u>conceal himself</u>.

3) Jekyll doesn't usually invite friends, like Utterson, into his laboratory, but hosts lively <u>dinner parties</u> in the main house. The laboratory is described as a "<u>dingy windowless structure</u>" — perfect for stopping other people from looking inside.

> **Character — Jekyll**
>
> The laboratory also <u>symbolises</u> Jekyll's <u>shame</u>. He transforms it from a place of ordinary <u>science</u> into one of <u>dark experiments</u>. At the end of the novel, he locks himself in the laboratory and dies there, as if he cannot face the world's <u>judgement</u>.

4) After Carew's murder, Utterson visits Jekyll in his laboratory. As he passes through the lecture theatre, he feels a "<u>sense of strangeness</u>". This adds to the <u>mystery</u> associated with this part of the building.

> Jekyll's house becomes <u>more sinister</u> as Hyde becomes more powerful. It becomes a "house of <u>voluntary bondage</u>". This suggests that Jekyll has <u>chosen</u> to lock himself in the house, just as he has tried to lock <u>Hyde</u> away within himself — he sees the house as <u>protection</u>, where he can <u>hide</u> his secrets.

Some objects also have symbolic meaning

© Nick Collinge @ Love It Studios

1) The <u>possessions</u> in Hyde's house in Soho belong to Jekyll. These expensive objects are a symbol of the <u>respectable</u> <u>gentleman</u> in the <u>rougher part</u> of the city.

2) The <u>cane</u> that Hyde uses to murder Carew was a <u>gift</u> from Utterson. It's a symbol of the Victorian <u>gentleman</u>, but it also demonstrates Stevenson's point that <u>civilised</u> people are capable of <u>violent</u> crimes.

3) Jekyll's <u>cheque book</u> initially gets him out of difficulty — he pays off the family of the girl he trampled as Hyde. However, after murdering Carew, he burns the cheque book. This shows that money <u>can't help him</u> to deal with a scandal of this scale.

4) The <u>mirror</u> is also a symbolic object. Jekyll's reflection as Hyde emphasises the fact that Hyde is his <u>double</u> (see p.48).

Write about the effect of settings on the reader...

Hyde's not the kind of chap you want to meet in a dark alley, but Stevenson's descriptions make it sound like he could be in <u>any</u> dark alley. And with a dense fog closing in, you wouldn't even hear him coming...

Language and Dialogue

All the prim and proper language in the novel can be off-putting, but stick with it — it's there for a reason.

The gentlemen's dialogue reflects their anxieties

The gentlemanly characters in *Jekyll and Hyde* often hide their anxieties behind polite dialogue:

Utterson	Utterson's dialogue is mostly rational and formal. He's keen to avoid discussing a scandal, so he uses vague phrases like "Tut-tut" rather than give an actual opinion. Utterson can be forceful when he needs to be, such as when he pushes Jekyll for "one word more" about his will. His language can also be humorous, for example when he says, "If he be Mr Hyde... I shall be Mr Seek."
Jekyll	Jekyll's dialogue is very guarded — he's always trying to avoid questions. He often chooses silence over speaking, for example, when Utterson asks him about his will, he shuts his mouth tight and nods. When Hyde becomes more powerful than Jekyll, his formal, guarded language breaks down. He has a "feverish" manner, speaks in a "changed voice", and stutters, "I have — I have."
Lanyon	To begin with, Lanyon's dialogue is jolly and "theatrical". He makes a joke about being one of Jekyll's oldest friends, and "chuckled". He also voices opinions and criticisms, accusing Jekyll of "unscientific balderdash" with a "little spirt of temper". Later, Lanyon's language becomes vague — "I saw what I saw, I heard what I heard". He's so disturbed by what he's seen that he refuses to write it down.

Poole's dialogue reflects his social class

1) Poole always refers to Utterson as "Mr Utterson" or "sir", and to Jekyll as "master". This demonstrates his role as a servant.

> In contrast, Utterson sometimes refers to Jekyll as "Harry" (a common nickname for 'Henry'). This shows that the two men are good friends and of the same class.

2) Poole's dialogue is often colloquial. When Utterson asks if Jekyll trusts Hyde, Poole replies, "Yes, sir, he do indeed." This non-standard grammar stands out sharply from the rest of Utterson's narrative, and suggests that he's less educated.

3) Poole doesn't conceal his emotions in the same way as the gentlemen do. His speech is anxious when he speaks to Utterson about his suspicions, and he shouts at the other servants with "ferocity".

Hyde's dialogue is uncivilised, like him

1) Hyde's speech is angry — when he first meets Utterson, he speaks "with a flush of anger." Utterson scolds him for not using "fitting language." Utterson is alarmed by Hyde's open emotion.

2) Hyde's dialogue is less polite. His sentences are short and direct, and he uses blunt questions, such as "What do you want?" Utterson finds this rude, because it's not how gentlemen talk.

3) Hyde has a "whispering and somewhat broken voice". This associates him with secrecy.

4) He also makes inhuman noises, like "hissing", and screams in an "animal terror". This suggests that he's not fully human.

Language and Dialogue

The language in the main narrative is mostly formal...

1) Stevenson writes most of the novel from Utterson's <u>perspective</u>. This narrative is mostly written in <u>formal</u>, <u>controlled</u> language. This reflects Utterson's <u>personality</u>.

2) The plot details are presented in an <u>orderly</u> fashion. When searching Jekyll's cabinet, the sentences are organised with <u>conjunctions</u> and <u>prepositions</u> such as "next", "on" and "at". The language of the narrative is as <u>organised</u> as Utterson himself.

Prepositions are words that tell you when or where something is in relation to something else.

3) The restrained language makes the <u>content</u> of the novel more <u>shocking</u> in contrast — it makes the moments of violence <u>stand out</u>. For example, when Poole breaks down the door to the cabinet, there's a sense of sudden <u>noise</u> and <u>exclamations</u>.

...but it is also very descriptive

Although the language in the main narrative is mostly <u>formal</u> and <u>controlled</u>, Stevenson uses passages of <u>description</u> to paint a <u>vivid picture</u> and bring events <u>alive</u> for the reader.

Similes	Metaphors	Personification
<u>Hyde</u> is constantly described using similes. He is "like a madman", "like a rat" and "like Satan." Characters can only <u>compare</u> Hyde to other things — they can't <u>accurately</u> describe him. This presents him as <u>mysterious</u> and <u>threatening</u>.	London is described as a "<u>drowned city</u>". This gives the impression that it's <u>smothered</u> by the dense fog. The streets are also described as "<u>arteries</u>", which makes the city seem like a <u>living body</u>.	The back of Jekyll's <u>laboratory</u> is personified. It "thrust forward" onto the pleasant street around it, and has "a blind forehead". This makes the building seem like a <u>rude</u> and <u>secretive</u> person, which represents <u>Hyde</u>, the person Jekyll has created there.

Stevenson uses double meanings to create secrecy

1) Stevenson emphasises the theme of <u>duality</u> by using words that can have more than one <u>meaning</u>. This adds to the atmosphere of <u>uncertainty</u>, and the <u>tension</u> between what is and isn't <u>real</u>.

2) For example, when Hyde disappears after Carew's murder, it's "<u>as if he never existed</u>". On the surface, this means Utterson is puzzled by Hyde's disappearance. If you read more closely, it's <u>actually true</u> — Hyde <u>has</u> never existed, because he's part of Jekyll. It's a <u>hidden clue</u> for the reader.

Theme — Secrecy

Jekyll's friends <u>don't realise</u> there's a <u>deeper meaning</u> to what he says, which helps to hide his <u>secret</u>. For example, when Jekyll says he will never set eyes on Hyde again, Utterson doesn't realise he's talking about looking in a mirror.

EXAM TIP

Write about the language of a variety of characters...

Don't get me wrong, the gentlemen's language is really important. But sticking in a bit about the language of other characters, like Poole and Hyde, will show the examiner that you know the novel really well.

'Jekyll and Hyde' as a Gothic Novel

The Gothic novel is a specific type of fiction which contains elements of horror and mystery. Gothic novels include Mary Shelley's *Frankenstein,* Bram Stoker's *Dracula* and Emily Brontë's *Wuthering Heights.*

'Jekyll and Hyde' has many features of a Gothic novel

Gothic novels often deal with <u>human emotion</u>, <u>mystery</u> and <u>supernatural</u> goings-on:

Mysterious settings	Stevenson's descriptions of the <u>dark</u>, <u>deserted</u> London streets, the "<u>fogged</u> city moon" and the <u>objects</u> in Jekyll's laboratory are all mysterious.
Disturbing secrets	Jekyll's <u>secret alter ego</u> is disturbing — Hyde commits horrific crimes, and inspires terror in everyone who meets him.
Dreams and visions	Utterson has a terrifying vision in which he is "<u>haunted</u>" by a faceless figure. It's a <u>frightening mixture</u> of Enfield's story and Utterson's own fears.
The supernatural	Jekyll's scientific experiments are "<u>mystic and the transcendental</u>". Lanyon describes <u>Hyde's transformation</u> in a way that seems <u>impossible</u> — his features "seemed to melt and alter". This suggests that Hyde isn't part of <u>this world</u>.
The double	The novel rests on the idea of man's double nature. As well as <u>Jekyll's</u> obvious duality, <u>other characters</u> and settings have two sides.

In Gothic novels, a double is a <u>pair</u> of characters. Sometimes these are <u>two separate people</u>, such as Victor Frankenstein and his creature in *Frankenstein.* In other books, they're <u>two sides</u> of the <u>same person</u>, such as Jekyll and Hyde.

The Gothic novel was popular in the late Victorian period

1) Traditionally, Gothic novels were set in <u>haunted buildings</u> or <u>abandoned castles</u>, in <u>faraway places</u> like medieval Europe. In the late Victorian period, this <u>changed</u> to focus on more modern and familiar settings. *Jekyll and Hyde* takes place in Victorian London.

2) Gothic novels usually featured an <u>evil character or villain</u>. In *Jekyll and Hyde*, the wicked character is actually <u>part</u> of a respectable man.

These changes made sure that Gothic novels were <u>still frightening</u> for Victorian readers. Stories about openly evil people in faraway places were easier to <u>dismiss</u>. The plot of *Jekyll and Hyde* is still too strange to be believed, but horrible deeds committed by <u>apparently civilised people</u> in <u>normal places</u> were more <u>terrifying</u>.

© MGM / Photofest

"The figure...haunted the lawyer all night"

If a scary story is set in some old castle half way up a French mountain, it's not as worrying for the Victorian gentleman reading by the fire. But if it's set in London, and the villain is a gentleman just like him — well...

Practice Questions

Congratulations, you've reached the end of a section. Guess what's coming next. Yes, it's another round of Practice Questions. This first page should get you warmed up nicely and thinking back to all the writer's techniques we've just covered. Make sure you can answer them all before you move on to the longer questions.

Quick Questions

1) Which character's experiences does the main narrative follow?

2) a) What is an embedded narrative?
   b) Give one example of an embedded narrative in *Jekyll and Hyde*.

3) Give one example of a letter that adds intrigue in *Jekyll and Hyde*.

4) Find a quote from the novel where the streets of London are described as:
   a) foggy
   b) empty
   c) dark

5) Give one example of an object from the novel that has symbolic meaning.

6) Which character's dialogue matches each of these descriptions?
   a) It's very guarded for most of the novel, but breaks down towards the end.
   b) It's mostly formal and rational, but can be forceful, and is sometimes humorous.
   c) It's initially jolly and theatrical, but becomes vague and disturbed.

7) a) How is Poole's language different from the gentlemen's language?
   b) How is Hyde's language different from the gentlemen's language?

8) Find an example of personification in the novel, and briefly explain its effect.

9) Find a quote that shows that the setting of *Jekyll and Hyde* is mysterious.

Practice Questions

The clue is in the name with these In-depth Questions — they need a little more thought than the ones on the previous page. Try to write about a paragraph for each one, and remember to use quotes and examples from the text to support your answers. You never know, you might be able to use them as part of an essay one day.

In-depth Questions

1) Describe two effects of using embedded narratives in the novel.

2) Of all the letters included in the narrative, which do you think is the most important? Explain your answer.

    For the purposes of this question, don't count Lanyon and Jekyll's narratives as letters.

3) Describe the importance of the novel's title and the chapter titles. Explain the effect of these.

4) What is the effect of the fog in the novel?

5) In what ways does Jekyll's house symbolise his character? Use quotes from the text to support your answer.

6) How does Stevenson use dialogue to develop his characters in the novel?

7) When he describes seeing Hyde, Poole says "the hair stood upon my head like quills." What is the effect of this simile?

    'Quills' are a bird's wing and tail feathers, or the spines of an animal like a hedgehog.

8) How is the idea of 'the double' used in *Jekyll and Hyde*? Mention at least two ways.

9) Give one example which shows how *Jekyll and Hyde* has features of the traditional Gothic novel and give one example which shows how it is different.

Practice Questions

You've reached the grand finale, folks — the Exam-style Questions. There's no better feeling than turning over an exam paper and realising you've answered a question (or a similar one) before.* Time to increase your chances of experiencing this glorious moment. Try some of these under exam conditions, too — practice makes perfect.

Exam-style Questions

1) Using the extract below as a starting point, explain how Stevenson creates mysterious settings.

> Taken from 'Search for Mr Hyde'
>
> From that time forward, Mr Utterson began to haunt the door in the bystreet of shops. In the morning before office hours, at noon when business was plenty and time scarce, at night under the face of the fogged city moon, by all lights and at all hours of solitude or concourse[1], the lawyer was to be found on his chosen post.
>
> "If he be Mr Hyde," he had thought, "I shall be Mr Seek."
>
> And at last his patience was rewarded. It was a fine dry night; frost in the air; the streets as clean as a ballroom floor; the lamps, unshaken by any wind, drawing a regular pattern of light and shadow. By ten o'clock, when the shops were closed, the bystreet was very solitary and, in spite of the low growl of London from all round, very silent. Small sounds carried far; domestic sounds out of the houses were clearly audible on either side of the roadway; and the rumour of the approach of any passenger preceded him by a long time. Mr Utterson had been some minutes at his post, when he was aware of an odd, light footstep drawing near. In the course of his nightly patrols, he had long grown accustomed to the quaint effect with which the footfalls of a single person, while he is still a great way off, suddenly spring out distinct from the vast hum and clatter of the city. Yet his attention had never before been so sharply and decisively arrested; and it was with a strong, superstitious prevision[2] of success that he withdrew into the entry of the court.
>
> [1] *concourse — crowd or gathering*
> [2] *prevision — foresight or prophecy*

2) Describe the narrative structure of *Jekyll and Hyde* and explain its effect on the reader.

3) Explore the effects of Stevenson's use of symbolism in the novel.

4) Read the passage in 'The Last Night' that begins "Mr Utterson's nerves, at this unlooked-for termination..." and ends "it doesn't commend itself to reason".
   How does the language of this passage create an atmosphere of tension and secrecy?

---

*There are actually many better feelings, like winning a million pounds or getting a new puppy, but that's by the bye.

Exam Preparation

Getting to know the text will put you at a massive advantage in the exam. It's not enough just to read it though — you've got to get to grips with the nitty-gritty bits. It's all about gathering evidence...

The exam questions will test four main skills

You will need to show the examiner that you can:

1) Write about the text in a thoughtful way — picking out appropriate examples and quotations to back up your opinions.

2) Identify and explain features of the text's form, structure and language. Show how the author uses these to create meanings and effects.

3) Relate the text to its cultural, social and historical background.

4) Write in a clear, well-structured way. 5% of the marks in your English Literature exams are for spelling, punctuation and grammar. Make sure that your writing is as accurate as possible.

Preparation is important

1) It's important to cover all the different sections of this book in your revision. You need to make sure you understand the text's context, plot, characters, themes and writer's techniques.

2) In the exam, you'll need to bring together your ideas about these topics to answer the question quickly.

3) Think about the different characters and themes in the text, and write down some key points and ideas about each one. Then, find some evidence to support each point — this could be something from any of the sections in this book. You could set out your evidence in a table like this:

Theme: Dual Nature of Man	
Repressed desires	Jekyll ashamed of his desires, separates them into Hyde. Dangers of repression seen in Jekyll's loss of control.
Primitive side of man	Hyde represents the primitive, uncivilised side of Jekyll. Compared to rat and ape. Darwin.
Hypocrisy of upper classes	Stevenson criticises the way people put on respectable appearances while sinning in secret.
Setting	Jekyll's sinister lab vs. his handsome home. Hyde's house in "dingy" Soho — located in respectable West End.
Language of battle	There's a "war" within Jekyll between his good side and his bad side.

Preparing to succeed — a cunning plot indeed...

Knowing the plot inside out will be unbelievably helpful in the exam. It'll help you to stay calm and make sure you write a brilliant answer that positively glitters with little gems of evidence. The exam's just a chance for you to show off...

The Exam Question

This page deals with how to approach an exam question. The stuff below will help you get started on a scorching exam answer, more scorching than, say, a phoenix cooking fiery fajitas in a flaming furnace.

Read the question carefully and underline key words

1) The style of question you'll get depends on which <u>exam board</u> you're taking.

2) Read all the <u>instructions</u> carefully. Make sure you know <u>how many</u> questions you need to answer and <u>how much time</u> you should spend answering each one.

3) If the question has <u>more than one part</u>, look at the total number of marks for each bit. This should help you to plan your <u>time</u> in the exam.

4) <u>Read</u> the question at least <u>twice</u> so you completely understand it. <u>Underline</u> the key words. If you're given an <u>extract</u>, underline <u>important</u> words or phrases in that too.

Henry didn't read the weather report carefully enough when planning his weekend activities.

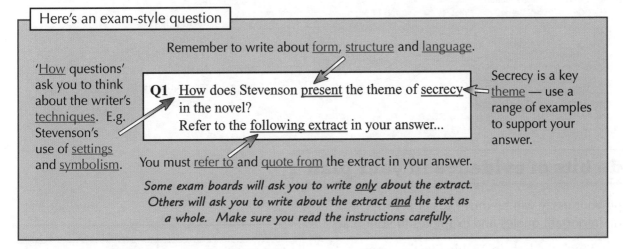

Here's an exam-style question

Remember to write about <u>form</u>, <u>structure</u> and <u>language</u>.

'<u>How</u> questions' ask you to think about the writer's <u>techniques</u>. E.g. Stevenson's use of <u>settings</u> and <u>symbolism</u>.

Q1 <u>How</u> does Stevenson <u>present</u> the theme of <u>secrecy</u> in the novel?
Refer to the <u>following extract</u> in your answer...

Secrecy is a key <u>theme</u> — use a range of examples to support your answer.

You must <u>refer to</u> and <u>quote from</u> the extract in your answer.

Some exam boards will ask you to write <u>only</u> about the extract. Others will ask you to write about the extract <u>and</u> the text as a whole. Make sure you read the instructions carefully.

Get to know exam language

Some <u>words</u> come up time and again in <u>exam questions</u>. Have a look at some <u>specimen</u> questions, pick out words that are <u>often used</u> in questions and make sure that you <u>understand</u> what they mean. You could <u>write a few down</u> whilst you're revising. For example:

Question Word	You need to...
Explore / Explain	Show <u>how</u> the writer deals with a <u>theme</u>, <u>character</u> or <u>idea</u>. Make several <u>different</u> points to answer the question.
How does	Think about the <u>techniques</u> or <u>literary features</u> that the author uses to get their point across.
Give examples	Use <u>direct quotes</u> and describe <u>events</u> from the text in your own words.
Refer to	Read the question so that you know if you need to write about just an <u>extract</u>, or an extract and the <u>rest of the text</u>.

The advice squad — the best cops in the NYPD...

Whatever question you're asked in the exam, your answer should touch on the main characters, themes, structure and language of the text. All the stuff we've covered in the rest of the book in fact. It's so neat, it's almost like we planned it.

Planning Your Answer

I'll say this once — and then I'll probably repeat it several times — it is absolutely, completely, totally and utterly essential that you make a plan before you start writing. Only a fool jumps right in without a plan...

Plan your answer before you start

1) If you plan, you're less likely to forget something <u>important</u>.

2) A good plan will help you <u>organise</u> your ideas — and write a good, <u>well-structured</u> essay.

3) Write your plan at the <u>top of your answer booklet</u> and draw a <u>neat line</u> through it when you've finished.

4) <u>Don't</u> spend <u>too long</u> on your plan. It's only <u>rough work</u>, so you don't need to write in full sentences. Here are a few <u>examples</u> of different ways you can plan your answer:

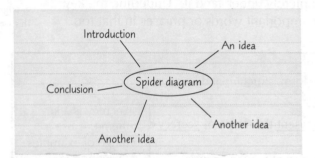

Bullet points...

- Introduction...
- An idea...
- The next idea...
- Another idea...
- Yet another idea...
- Conclusion...

Include bits of evidence in your plan

1) <u>Writing</u> your essay will be much <u>easier</u> if you include <u>important quotes</u> and <u>examples</u> in your plan.

2) You could include them in a <u>table</u> like this one:

3) <u>Don't</u> spend <u>too long</u> writing out quotes though. It's just to make sure you <u>don't forget</u> anything when you write your answer.

A point...	Quote to back this up...
Another point...	Quote...
A different point...	Example...
A brand new point...	Quote...

Structure your answer

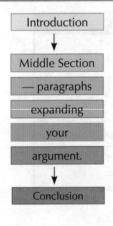

1) Your <u>introduction</u> should give a brief answer to the question you're writing about. Make it clear how you're going to <u>tackle the topic</u>.

2) The <u>middle section</u> of your essay should explain your answer in detail and give evidence to back it up. Write a <u>paragraph</u> for each point you make. Make sure you <u>comment</u> on your evidence and <u>explain how</u> it helps to <u>prove</u> your point.

3) Remember to write a <u>conclusion</u> — a paragraph at the end which <u>sums up</u> your <u>main points</u>. There's <u>more</u> about introductions and conclusions on the <u>next page</u>.

Dirk finally felt ready to tackle the topic.

To plan or not to plan, that is the question...

The answer is yes, yes, a thousand times yes. Often students dive right in, worried that planning will take up valuable time. But 5 minutes spent organising a well-structured answer is loads better than pages of waffle. Mmm waffles.

Section Six — Exam Advice

Writing Introductions and Conclusions

Now you've made that plan that I was banging on about on the last page, you'll know what your main points are. This is going to make writing your introduction and conclusion as easy as pie.

Get to the point straight away in your introduction

1) First, you need to <u>work out</u> what the question is <u>asking you</u> to do:

> How is the character of Dr Lanyon important to the novel?

> The question is <u>asking you</u> to think about the <u>role</u> of <u>Dr Lanyon</u> in the text.
> Plan your essay by thinking about <u>how</u> this character <u>links</u> to the text's overall <u>message</u>.

2) When you've <u>planned</u> your essay, you should <u>begin</u> by giving a <u>clear answer</u> to the <u>question</u> in a sentence or two. Use the <u>rest</u> of the <u>introduction</u> to <u>develop</u> this idea. Try to include the <u>main paragraph ideas</u> that you have listed in your plan, but <u>save</u> the <u>evidence</u> for later.

3) You could also use the <u>introduction</u> to give your <u>opinion</u>. Whatever you do, make sure your introduction makes it <u>clear</u> how your answer <u>fits the question</u>.

Your conclusion must answer the question

1) The <u>most important</u> thing you have to do at the <u>end</u> of your writing is to <u>summarise</u> your <u>answer</u> to the question.

2) It's your <u>last chance</u> to persuade the examiner, so make your <u>main point</u> again.

3) Use your <u>last sentence</u> to really <u>impress</u> the <u>examiner</u> — it will make your essay <u>stand out</u>. You could <u>develop</u> your own <u>opinion</u> of the text or <u>highlight</u> which of your <u>points</u> you thought was the most <u>interesting</u>.

The examiner was struggling to see the answer clearly.

Use the question words in your introduction and conclusion

1) Try to use <u>words</u> or <u>phrases</u> from the <u>question</u> in your introduction and conclusion.

> How does Stevenson use setting in the novel?

2) This will show the examiner that you're <u>answering the question</u>.

> Stevenson uses setting in 'Jekyll and Hyde' to create symbolic meaning. The settings link to the main themes of the novel, such as duality and secrecy.

The first line of the introduction gives a clear answer, which will lead on to the rest of the essay.

3) This will also help you keep the question <u>fresh in your mind</u> so your answer doesn't <u>wander off-topic</u>.

I've come to the conclusion that I really like pie...

To conclude, the introduction eases the examiner in gently, whilst the conclusion is your last chance to impress. But remember — the examiner doesn't want to see any new points lurking in those closing sentences.

Writing Main Paragraphs

So we've covered the beginning and the end, now it's time for the meaty bit. The roast beef in between the prawn cocktail and the treacle tart. This page is about how to structure your paragraphs. It's quite simple...

P.E.E.D. is how to put your argument together

Remember to start a new paragraph every time you make a new point.

1) P.E.E.D. stands for: Point, Example, Explain, Develop.

2) Begin each paragraph by making a point. Then give an example from the text (either a quote or a description). Next, explain how your example backs up your point.

3) Finally, try to develop your point by writing about its effect on the reader, how it links to another part of the text or what the writer's intention is in including it.

Use short quotes to support your ideas

1) Don't just use words from the novel to show what happens in the plot...

> Utterson rarely smiles. He has a "rugged countenance that was never lighted by a smile".

This just gives an example from the text without offering any explanation or analysis.

2) Instead, it's much better to use short quotes as evidence to support a point you're making.

3) It makes the essay structure clearer and smoother if most quotes are embedded in your sentences.

It's better to use short, embedded quotes as evidence. Then you can go on to explain them.

> Utterson's face is "never lighted by a smile" because he represses his emotions. As a model Victorian gentleman, he needs to appear respectable at all times, which means hiding any emotions he thinks might be judged as unseemly.

Get to know some literary language

1) Using literary terms in your answer will make your essay stand out — as long as you use them correctly.

2) When you're revising, think about literary terms that are relevant to the text and how you might include them in an essay. Take a look at the table below for some examples.

Literary Term	Definition	Example
Personification	A figure of speech that talks about a thing as if it's a person.	"a blind forehead of discoloured wall"
Simile	Compares one thing to another, often using 'like' and 'as'.	"that masked thing like a monkey"
Metaphor	Describing something by saying it is something else.	"the drowned city"

This page is so exciting — I nearly...

Now now, let's all be grown-ups and avoid the obvious joke. It's a good way of remembering how to structure your paragraphs though. Point, Example, Explain, Develop. Simple. Maybe we could make a rap or something... anyone?

In the Exam

Keeping cool in the exam can be tricky. But if you take in all the stuff on this page, you'll soon have it down to a fine art. Then you can stroll out of that exam hall with the swagger of an essay-writing master.

Don't panic if you make a mistake

1) Okay, so say you've timed the exam beautifully. Instead of putting your feet up on the desk for the last 5 minutes, it's a good idea to <u>read through</u> your <u>answers</u> and <u>correct any mistakes</u>...

2) If you want to get rid of a mistake, <u>cross it out</u>. <u>Don't scribble</u> it out as this can look messy. Make any corrections <u>neatly</u> and <u>clearly</u> instead of writing on top of the words you've already written.

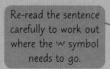

The author uses various literary ~~teknikues~~ techniques to explore this theme .

This is the clearest way to correct a mistake. Don't be tempted to try writing on top of the original word.

3) If you've <u>left out</u> a <u>word</u> or a <u>phrase</u> and you've got space to add it in <u>above</u> the line it's missing from, write the missing bit above the line with a '∧' to show exactly where it should go.

Re-read the sentence carefully to work out where the '∧' symbol needs to go.

The writer uses imagery to draw attention to this point.
                          ∧ and hyperbole

4) If you've left out whole <u>sentences</u> or <u>paragraphs</u>, write them in a <u>separate section</u> at the <u>end</u> of the essay. Put a <u>star</u> (*) next to both the <u>extra writing</u> and the <u>place</u> you want it to go.

Always keep an eye on the time

1) It's surprisingly <u>easy</u> to <u>run out of time</u> in exams. You've got to leave <u>enough time</u> to answer <u>all</u> the questions you're asked to do. You've also got to leave enough time to <u>finish</u> each essay properly — with a <u>clear ending</u>.

2) Here are some <u>tips</u> on how to <u>avoid</u> running out of time:

- Work out <u>how much time</u> you have for each part of your answer <u>before</u> you <u>start</u>.
- Take off a few minutes at the beginning to <u>plan</u>, and a <u>few minutes</u> at the end for your <u>conclusion</u>.
- Make sure you have a <u>watch</u> to <u>time yourself</u> — and keep checking it.
- Be <u>strict</u> with yourself — if you spend <u>too long</u> on one part of your answer, you may run out of time.
- If you're <u>running out of time</u>, keep <u>calm</u>, <u>finish</u> the <u>point</u> you're on and move on to your <u>conclusion</u>.

Stephanie never had a problem with keeping cool.

Treat an exam like a spa day — just relax...

Some people actually do lose the plot when they get into the exam. The trick is to keep calm and well... carry on. If you make sure you get your exam technique sorted, you'll be as relaxed as a sloth in a room full of easy chairs.

Sample Exam Question

And now the bit you've all been waiting for — a sample exam question and a lovely little plan.
Go and make yourself a cup of tea, then settle down and enjoy.

Here's a sample exam question...

Read this feisty exam question. That's the best way to start...

In the exam, you'll be given the full extract in the exam paper.

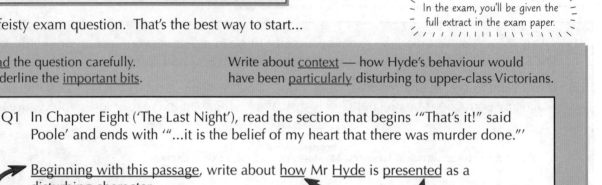

Read the question carefully.
Underline the important bits.

Write about context — how Hyde's behaviour would have been particularly disturbing to upper-class Victorians.

Q1   In Chapter Eight ('The Last Night'), read the section that begins '"That's it!" said Poole' and ends with '"...it is the belief of my heart that there was murder done."'

Beginning with this passage, write about how Mr Hyde is presented as a disturbing character.

You'll need to discuss the passage given in detail but you also need to refer to the rest of the book.

You need to think about what it is that makes Hyde disturbing. E.g. his actions, his appearance and other characters' reactions to him.

Think about how Stevenson uses language and dialogue to present the character of Mr Hyde.

Here's how you could plan your answer

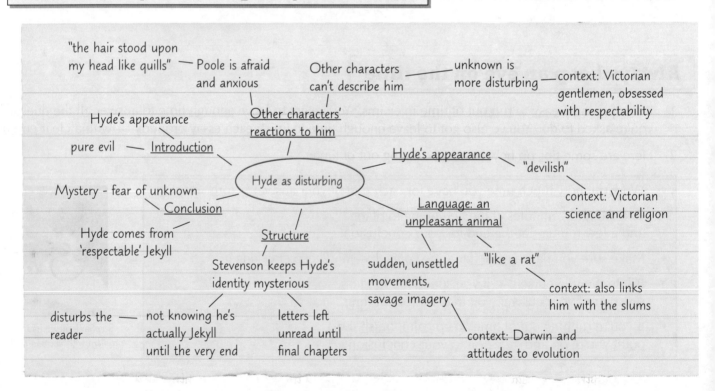

"the hair stood upon my head like quills" — Poole is afraid and anxious

Other characters can't describe him

unknown is more disturbing — context: Victorian gentlemen, obsessed with respectability

Hyde's appearance

pure evil — Introduction

Other characters' reactions to him

Hyde's appearance

"devilish"

Mystery - fear of unknown
Conclusion

Hyde as disturbing

Language: an unpleasant animal

context: Victorian science and religion

Hyde comes from 'respectable' Jekyll

Structure

Stevenson keeps Hyde's identity mysterious

sudden, unsettled movements, savage imagery

"like a rat"

context: also links him with the slums

disturbs the reader — not knowing he's actually Jekyll until the very end

letters left unread until final chapters

context: Darwin and attitudes to evolution

What do examiners eat? Why, egg-sam-wiches of course...

The most important thing to remember is DON'T PANIC. Take a deep breath, read the question, read it again, write a plan... take another deep breath... and start writing. Leave a few minutes at the end to check your answer too.

Worked Answer

These pages will show you how to take an OK answer and turn it into a really good one that will impress the examiner.

Use your introduction to get off to a good start

> These pages are all about how to word your sentences to impress the examiner, so we haven't included everything from the plan on page 58.

You might start with something like...

> Hyde is presented as a disturbing character in a number of ways, including his dialogue and appearance. Other characters' reactions to him also make Hyde seem sinister and unsettling.

1) This intro is okay. It acknowledges that Hyde is disturbing for different reasons.
2) It's also a good idea to use the key words in the question to give your essay focus and show the examiner you're on track and that you're thinking about the question from the start.
3) But there's still room for improvement...

> Stevenson uses a number of different techniques to present Hyde as a disturbing character in the extract: his appearance is startling, his movements are unsettling, and he is associated with the hidden dark side of Victorian society. Hyde has a disturbing presence because he is a purely evil character with no redeeming features. This makes him seem inhuman because human nature is made up of a balance of good and bad qualities.

This intro talks about the social and historical context.

This tells the examiner what the essay's about and shows that you've thought about your essay structure.

Develop each point with detailed comments and quotes

> Poole feels a sense of horror when he sees Hyde. His shock and confusion are shown by the fact he repeatedly asks questions. He even stops talking because he can't put what he saw into words.

1) This paragraph makes several different points about Poole's reaction to Hyde. But it doesn't develop the points fully by giving quotes or talking about the language used.
2) You should develop your points with detail and comments:

> Stevenson uses other characters' reactions to Hyde to demonstrate that he is a disturbing character. Poole is left afraid and anxious after his sighting of Hyde, and he is unable to finish the sentence that he begins with "And then...". This shows that his fear and confusion after seeing Hyde are strong enough to make him inarticulate. Similarly, Lanyon states that Hyde is "not easy to describe" and says that he can't "specify the point" about why Hyde is so unsettling. Stevenson is using these characters' reactions to suggest that Hyde is so disturbing that he's impossible to describe. The presentation of Hyde is particularly unnerving because he inspires deep-seated feelings of disgust and hatred in those who meet him, and yet this is not solely because of his appearance. There is something unnatural and frightening about Hyde that is impossible to identify or explain.

Start by introducing the main point of your paragraph.

Use evidence from the extract to back up your point. Then show how it links to rest of the text.

Explain how your evidence supports your original point.

Finally, develop your point by analysing the effect of Stevenson's writing on the reader.

Worked Answer

Link your points to the novel's context and themes

You need to link your points to both the question and the rest of the novel. Don't just focus on the extract.

> Stevenson uses animalistic language to make Hyde seem disturbing. Poole describes him as being like a "rat", which presents Hyde as the primitive side of Jekyll's respectable character.

1) This paragraph builds on the idea that Hyde is disturbing because he's less civilised.

2) However, you can improve it by discussing how this relates to the themes of the novel:

> Poole describes Hyde as "like a rat" and portrays him as "digging among the crates" and giving a "kind of cry". This animalistic imagery suggests that Hyde is savage and less civilised than Jekyll, a reputable, upper-class gentleman. This links to the wider theme that all humans have a dual nature: there's a constant struggle between the good, civilised side and the darker, more primitive side of man. Hyde's character is disturbing because it forces the reader to confront the frightening idea that they have a version of Mr Hyde within them.

It's a good idea to show the examiner you're aware of how the extract displays the themes of the novel.

Don't forget to explain how your points link to the exam question.

3) You could develop this by focusing on the context in which the novel was written:

Make sure your comments on context are linked closely to the text and the question.

> Upper-class Victorians, like Utterson and Jekyll, were very concerned with appearing respectable, so they struggled with the idea that people had a primitive side. They hid their darker, less respectable desires beneath a civilised exterior by following excessively strict codes of behaviour. The fact that Hyde is actually part of a well-respected Victorian gentleman would have been particularly disturbing to a Victorian audience.

Finish your essay in style

You could say:

> In conclusion, this extract shows that Hyde is a disturbing character through animalistic descriptions of his appearance and behaviour, as well as the effect he has on other characters.

1) This conclusion is okay, but it doesn't go into much detail about how Hyde is presented as disturbing.

2) So to make it really impressive you could say something like...

> Hyde is a disturbing character because he represents the evil side of human nature. This is demonstrated by Stevenson in various ways, including his use of animalistic language to describe Hyde and his depictions of other characters' inarticulate and repulsed reactions to Hyde. Hyde is capable of extreme cruelty, and the fact that his evil nature originates from Jekyll, a respectable gentleman, is highly disturbing. Hyde's wickedness hints at something beyond our understanding, which is truly frightening.

This shows that you've considered all the techniques Stevenson used

Make your last sentence really stand out — it's your last opportunity to impress the examiner.

Why do alligators write good essays? Their quotes are so snappy...

It seems like there's a lot to remember on these two pages, but there's not really. To summarise — write a scorching intro and a sizzling conclusion, make a good range of points (one per paragraph) and include plenty of examples. Easy.

Index

Index

The Characters in 'Dr Jekyll and Mr Hyde'

Phew! You should be an expert on *Dr Jekyll and Mr Hyde* by now. But if you want a bit of light relief and a quick recap of the novel's plot, sit yourself down and read through *Dr Jekyll and Mr Hyde — The Cartoon...*

Dr Jekyll

Mr Hyde

Mr Utterson

Dr Lanyon

Poole

Mr Enfield

Robert Louis Stevenson's 'Dr Jekyll and Mr Hyde'

ONE DAY, A LAWYER CALLED UTTERSON IS WALKING WITH HIS COUSIN, ENFIELD

By jingo, would you look at that horrible, dark door.

I know a story about that actually. Once upon a time...

Mr Utterson   Mr Enfield

"... I WAS WALKING DOWN THE STREET AT 3AM WHEN I SAW SOMETHING AWFUL..."

Ha ha ha!

Mr Hyde

STOMP! STOMP!

You scoundrel! You shan't get away with this!

Alright chump, name your price.

"WE WENT TO THE MYSTERIOUS DOOR. HYDE WENT INSIDE AND WHEN HE CAME OUT, HE GAVE THE VICTIM A CHEQUE."

Mystery Bank
PAY TO THE ORDER OF Trampled Girl & Family
Loads of dosh —
18—

Tut tut. Nasty business. What what.

Indeed. And the cheque was in someone else's name! Well, shouldn't gossip...

The shady door is a back entrance to Henry Jekyll's laboratory! Jekyll must've signed the cheque!

THAT EVENING IN UTTERSON'S STUDY...

Let's see...Last Will and Testament of Henry Jekyll...blah blah blah... "Hyde gets everything I own if I die." Good gravy! I simply must see Dr Lanyon about this.

Jekyll's Will

AT LANYON'S HOUSE...

I've fallen out with Jekyll. His science was getting a bit barmy.

Cripes. Have you heard anything about a chap called Hyde?

Nope, never heard of him.

Dr Lanyon

A FEW DAYS LATER...

Hyde, you ragamuffin!

Pah! How do you know my name?

My chum Jekyll.

Liar, liar! Pantaloons on fire!

AT JEKYLL'S HOUSE...

Since Jekyll's not home, tell me everything you can about this chap Hyde.

We have orders to obey him from Dr Jekyll himself. He has a key to the door and comes and goes as he wishes.

By gum! That crook Hyde must be blackmailing Jekyll!

Poole

TWO WEEKS LATER, AT JEKYLL'S...

Why have you and Lanyon fallen out?

I'm in a very strange position that I can't tell you anything whatsoever about. Except it's to do with Hyde. Stop asking questions.

Dr Jekyll

NEARLY A YEAR LATER...

Maid

I'm being attacked! If it's not too much trouble, send for help!

Danvers Carew

Letter for Utterson

NEXT MORNING

There's been a murder!

To the morgue! Well, once I've had my brekkie.

Danvers Carew, may he rest in peace. Wait a minute! That bloodied cane belongs to Hyde! Time to play Hyde and seek!

Ha ha ha!

AT HYDE'S...

Drat! Nothing here but burnt papers and the other half of the cane.

THAT AFTERNOON IN JEKYLL'S CABINET

I suppose you've heard about the murder. You haven't been protecting Hyde, have you?

I'm done with Hyde forever! I am 100% certain he's gone. I, er, can't tell you how I know that, but here's a letter he sent this morning saying that he's safe.

That's curious.

Have any letters been delivered here this morning?

No Sir.

That's also curious.

THAT EVENING AT UTTERSON'S HOUSE

Look at this letter.

Looks like Jekyll's writing.

Who would've *GUEST* it?

Even more curious. I do believe Jekyll is forging letters for Hyde!

Mr Guest

ETJH41